LEARN TO SPEAK AND WRITE GERMAN

Other Books on

LANGUAGE BOOKS

1. Learn to Speak and Write Arabic
2. Teach Yourself Spanish
3. Learn to Speak and Write Russian
4. Learn to Speak and Write Korean
5. French Made Easy
6. Learn to Speak and Write Hindi
7. Learn to Speak and Write Italian
8. Conversational Chinese
9. Learn to Speak and Write French
10. Learn to Speak and Write German
11. Learn to Speak and Write Spanish
12. Learn to Speak and Write Japanese

Lotus PRESS

Unit No. 220, 2nd Floor, 4735/22, Prakash Deep Building,
Ansari Road, Darya Ganj, New Delhi- 110002
Phone : 41325510, 9811838000
E-mail : lotuspress1984@gmail.com, www.lotuspress.co.in

LEARN TO SPEAK AND WRITE GERMAN

Sudhir Khanna

4735/22, Prakash Deep Building,
Ansari Road, Daryaganj,
New Delhi-110002

Lotus Press : Publishers & Distributors
Unit No. 220, 2nd Floor, 4735/22, Prakash Deep Building,
Ansari Road, Darya Ganj, New Delhi- 110002
Ph.: 41325510, 98118-38000
• E-mail : lotuspress1984@gmail.com
www.lotuspress.co.in

Learn to Speak and Write French

ISBN: 81-89093-85-1

Printed & Published by : **Lotus Press Publisher & Distributors,** New Delhi-02

Introduction To the Book..

Our books on **FOREIGN LANGUAGES** have been designed keeping in mind the increasing number of tourists, businessmen and others who visit Foreign countries very often.

These books can also serve as a basics for a complete study of these languages.

Learners who use these books can easily make themselves understood where these languages are spoken. By reading these books one is not required to learn a long list of grammatical rules. Because in these books small charts has been given to learn the grammer rules easily. Up-to date vocabulary has been given with special coverage of terms used in business trade & travel . Clear explanation of the different meanings of each word has been given so that learner does not face any problem in learning the words. The section on grammer-expanded & illustrated with clear, brief sample senteces & words-that will provide helpful guidence to all readers.

We, at Lotus Press, are pretty confident that these books will give the leaners a useful introduction to these languages. This can eventually lead the learners to achieve a complete mastery on their chosen language.

LEARN TO SPEAK AND WRITE IN **GERMAN**. Helps you to get familier with the German language and we, are sure once you have gone through this Book you will have a better understanding of the rules of German language you will be able to read & write German Properly. Anyone interested in doing business in Germany or wants to make career in German Language would find this book educative & helpful.

Rest & all is the will of our Lord.

—Publishers

◆ TABLE OF CONTENTS ◆

Lesson 1

German Alphabet

The alphabet is a very practical thing to learn. There are times when you may need to spell your name or other words on the phone. A **BMW** car is pronounced BAY-EM-VAY in German. A **VW** is a FOW-VAY. Many other German words are reduced to letters in the same way: **Lkw** *(truck, ELL-KA-VAY)*, **Pkw** *(car, PAY-KA-VAY)*, **ICE** *(high-speed train, EE-TSAY-AY)*. After studying this chart, you will be able to correctly pronounce the German alphabets easily and properly.

Letter	*Pronunciation*	*Examples*
A a	**aa**	ab (*from*)
Ä ä	**ay**	der Äther (*ether*), die Fähre (*ferry*)
B b	**bay**	bei (*at, near*), das Buch (*book*)
C c	**tsay**	die City (*down town*), der Computer
D d	**day**	durch (through), dunkel (*dark*)

E e	**ay**	elf (*eleven*), wer (*who*), er (*he*)
F f	**ef**	faul (*lazy*), der Feind (*enemy*)
G g	**gay**	das Gehirn (*brain*), gleich (*same, equal*)
H h	**haa**	die Hand (hand), halb (*half*)
I i	**ee**	der Igel (*hedgehog*), immer (*always*)
J j	**yot**	das Jahr (*year*), jung (*young*)
K k	**kaa**	der Kalender (*calen dar*), kennen (*to know*)
L l	**el**	langsam (*slow, slowly*)
M m	**em**	mein (*my*), der Mann (*man*)
N n	**en**	der Nacht (*night*), nein (*no*), nicht (*not*)
O o	**oh**	das Ohr (*ear*), die Oper (*opera*)
Ö ö	**ay***	Österreich (*Austria*)
P p	**pay**	das Papier (*paper*), positiv (*positive*)
Q q	**koo**	die Quelle (*source*), quer (*crosswise*)
R r	**err**	das Rathaus (*city hall*), rechts (*on the right*)
S s	**es**	die Sache (*matter*), das Salz (*salt*)

T t	**tay**	der Tag (*day*), das Tier (*animal*)
U u	**oo**	die U-Bahn (*subway, metro*)
Ü ü	**ee***	über *(over, about)*, die Tür *(door)*
V v	**fow**	der Vater (*father*), vier (*four*)
W w	**vay**	wenn (*if, when*), die Woche (*week*)
X x	**ix**	x-mal (*umpteen times*), das Xylophone
Y y	**ipsilon***	die yacht (yacht)
Z z	**tset**	zahlen (*to pay)*, die *(pizza)*, zu (*to, too*)

Pronounce while rounding lips

Lesson 2

Diphthongs and Consonant Pairs

German is a much more phonetically consistent language than English. This means that German words usually sound the way they are spelled—with consistent sounds for any given spelling. (*e.g., the German* ***ei*** *- as in nein - spelling is always sounded EYE, whereas German* ***ie*** *- as in Sie - always has the EE sound.)* No need to learn exceptions like English 'i before e, except after c'. In German, the rare exceptions are usually foreign words from English, French or other languages. Any student of German should learn the sounds associated with certain spellings as soon as possible. Knowing them, you will be able to correctly pronounce even German words you have never seen before!

Now that you know how to pronounce the letters of the alphabet in German, we will advance to the next stage. First, let us talk about some terminology. It is helpful to know, for instance, what diphthongs and paired consonants are.

Diphthongs

A diphthong (*Greek di, two + phthongos, sound, voice*) is a combination of two vowels that blend and are sounded together. Instead of being pronounced separately, the two letters have one sound or pronunciation. An example would be the **au** combination. The diphthong **au** in German always has the sound OW, as in English 'how' *(the 'ou' being an English diphthong; the* ***au*** *is also part of the German word* ***autsch****, which is pronounced almost the same as 'ouch' in English!)* Obviously, this kind of information is very useful to know when you are trying to pronounce German. In the chart below, we present more examples of German diphthongs.

Grouped or Paired Consonants

While diphthongs are always vowel pairs; German also has many common **grouped** or **paired consonants** that have a consistent pronunciation as well. An example of this would be **st**, a very common combination of the consonants s and t, found in many German words. In standard German, the **st** combination at the beginning of a word is always pronounced like SCHT and *not* like the **st** found in English 'stay' or 'stone'. Therefore, a German word such as **Stein** *(stone something like)* is pronounced SCHTINE, with an initial SCH-sound, as in 'show'. You will find more examples of paired consonants in the chart below.

Diphthongs

Diphthong Double Vowels	Aussprache Pronunciation	Beispiele / Examples
ai / ei	**eye**	bei (*at, near*), das Ei (*egg*), der Mai (*May*)

au	**ow**	auch (*also*), das Auge (*eye*), aus (*out of*)
eu / äu	**oy**	Häuser (*houses*), Europa (*Europe*), neu (*new*)
ie	**ee**	bieten (*to offer*), nie (*never*), Sie (*you all*) (Formal).

Grouped Consonants

Konsonant Consonant	**Aussprache Pronunciation**	**Beispiele / Examples**
ck	**k**	dick (*fat, thick*), der Schock (*shock*)
ch	>>	After a, o, u and au, pronounced like the guttural ch in Scottish 'loch' - das Buch (*book*), auch (*also*). Otherwise it is a palatal sound as in: mich (me), welche (*which*), wirklich (*really*). TIP: If no air is passing over your tongue when you say a ch-sound, you aren't saying it correctly. No true equivalent in English. Although ch doesn't usually have a hard k

		sound, there are exceptions: choir (choir), Christoph, Chaos (chaos), Orchestra (orchestra), Wachs (*wax*)
pf	**pf**	Both letters are *quickly* pronounced as a combined puff-sound: das Pferd (*horse*), der Pfennig (pfennig). If this is difficult for you, an sound will work, but try to do it !
ph	**f**	das Alphabet (alphabet), phonetic (phonetic)- Some words formerly spelled with ph are now spelled with f: das Telefon, das Foto
qu	**kv**	die Qual *(anguish, pain)*, die Quittung *(receipt)*
sch	**sh**	schön *(pretty)*, die Schule *(school)* - The German sch combination is never split, whereas sh usually is (*Grashalm- Blade of grass, Gras/Halm; but die Show, a foreign word*).

sp / st	**shp / sht**	At the start of a word, the s in sp/st has a sch sound as in English 'show, she'. sprechen (*to speak*), stehen (*to stand*)
th	**th**	das Theater (*THAY-AATER*), das Thema (*THAY- MAA*) - topic. Always sounds like a t (*THAY*). has the English th Sound !

Lesson 3

Pronunciation

A German Pronunciation Guide.

In this part of the German Pronunciation Guide, we offer more tips and point out some hidden dangers caused by interference from English.

Letter sounds in words

Previously, we showed you how to pronounce the letters of the alphabet and certain letter combinations in German. Now we want to concentrate on how to pronounce other letters and letter combinations found within German words. For instance, a 'd' at the end of a German word usually has a hard 't' sound in German, not the hard 'd' sound of English. That is just one example of the many found in the chart on the next page.

Similar words

In addition, the fact that English and German words are often identical or very similar in spelling, can lead to pronunciation errors. We will show you some mistakes you can avoid in the second chart below, but here are two 'dangerous' examples: bomb/**Bombe** and pizza/**Pizza**. The German word for bomb is pronounced BOM-buh (*with both the 'm' and the final 'e' sounded*). A German pizza sounds like PITS-uh, not PEET-sa!

Here are some more examples of German pronunciation pitfalls:

Letters in words

Spelling Pronunciation	**Aussprache Examples**	**Beispiele /**
final b	**p**	**Lob** *(LOHP)*
final d	**t**	**Freund** (*FROYNT*), Wald (*VALT*)
final g	**k**	**genug** (*geh-NOOK*)
silent h	-	**gehen** (*GAY-hen*), **sehen** (*ZAY-hen*) When h follows a vowel, it is silent. When it precedes a vowel (*Hund*), the h is pronounced.
German v	**f**	**Vater** (*FAHT-er*) In some foreign, non-Germanic words with v, the v is pronounced as in English: Vase *(VAH-zuh)*, Villa *(VILL-ah)*

German w	**v**	Wunder (*VOON-der*)
German z	**ts**	Zeit (*TSITE*), like ts in 'cats'; never like an English soft z (*as in 'zoo'*)

Similar Words	**Words Pronunciation**	**Pitfalls**
Word	**Pronunciation**	**Comments**
Bombe bomb	**BOM-buh**	Both the m and the e are sounded
Genie genius	**Gay-NEE**	The g is soft, like the s sound in 'leisure'
Nation nation	**NAHT-see-ohn**	The German -tion suffix is pronounced TSEE-ohn
Papier paper	**pah-PEER**	Stress on the last syllable
Pizza pizza	**PITS-ah**	The i is a short vowel because of the double z

Lesson 4

Personal Pronouns

German Personal Pronouns and Formal versus Familiar 'you'

The German personal pronouns (*er, sie, es, du, wir, usw.*) work in much the same way as their English equivalents (*he, she, it, you, we, etc.*). When we get to verb conjugation later, these words will be a key element that you should know very well. Even here, we have included some sample verb phrases for many of the pronouns.

A special word about 'you'! German, much more than English, makes a clear distinction between formal you (***Sie***) and familiar you (*first name, **du***) in social situations. In this regard, Germans tend to be more formal than English-speakers and use first names only after a long period of getting to know each other (sometimes years). This is a good example of how language and culture are intertwined, and you need to be aware of this to avoid embarrassing yourself and others. In the table below, the familiar 'you' forms ***(du, ihr)*** are marked with the abbreviation 'fam'. to distinguish them from the formal 'you' ***(Sie)***.

German has three different forms of **sie**! Often the only way to tell which one is meant is to notice the verb ending and/or the context in which the pronoun is used. Even the capitalised **Sie** (you, formal) is tricky if it appears at the beginning of a sentence. Lower-case **sie** can mean both 'she' and 'they': **sie ist** (*she is*), **sie sind** (*they are*).

German Pronouns

The pronouns listed below are in the Nominative (*subject*) case.

Nominative SingularPronoun	Pronoun	Sample Phrases
ich	**I**	Darf ich? (*May I?*) Ich bin 16 Jahre alt. (*I'm 16 years old.*) The pronoun ich is not capitalised except at the beginning of a sentence.
du	**you (fam.)**	Kommst **du** mit? *(Are you coming along?)*
er	**he**	Ist **er** da? *(Is he here?)*
sie	**she**	Ist **sie** da? *(Is she here?)*
es	**it**	Hast du **es**? *(Do you have it?)*
Sie	**you (formal)**	Kommen **Sie** heute? *(Are you coming today?)*

The pronoun Sie always takes a plural conjugation, but is also used for the formal 'you' singular.

Nominative Plural Pronoun	Pronoun	Sample Phrases
wir	**we**	**Wir** kommen am Dienstag. *(We're coming on Tuesday.)*
ihr	**you guys (fam.)**	You both Habt **ihr** das Geld? *(Do you guys have the money?)*
sie	**they**	**Sie** kommen heute. *(They're coming today.)* The pronoun sie in this sentence could also mean 'you' Sie. Only the context makes it clear which of the two is meant.
Sie	**you (plur.)**	Kommen **Sie** heute? *(Are you [all] coming today?)*

Lesson 5

Nouns and Gender

German nouns *(a person, place or thing, **Substantive**)* are very easy to spot: they always begin with a capital letter! **German is the only world language that capitalises all nouns**. Although there has been debate over the years about doing away with this rather inefficient practice, for now ALL German nouns must begin with a capital letter. Whether we are talking about a simple tree ***(ein Baum)*** or **Deutsche Bank**, any noun is capitalised in German.

The other important thing for English-speakers to understand about German nouns is the matter of gender. Just as we learned about the pronouns in the previous chapter, German nouns parallel he, she and it ***(er, sie, es)*** by also being masculine ***(der** - DARE)*, feminine ***(die** - DEE)* or neuter ***(das** - DAHSS)*. We can see the parallel very clearly by the ending letters for each article/pronoun: **der = er**, **die = sie**, **das = es**.

Der, **die** and **das** are the same as 'the' in English – the Definite Article. In German, the definite article is much more important than it is in English. For one thing, it is used more often. In English we might say: 'Nature is wonderful'. In German, the article would also be included: 'Die Natur ist wunderbar. So knowing which article to use becomes even more important!

The Indefinite Article *('a' or 'an' in English)* is **ein** or **eine** in German. **Ein** means 'one' and like the definite article; it indicates the gender of the noun it goes with ***(eine** or **ein**).* For a feminine noun, only **eine** can be used *(in the nominative case).* For masculine or neuter nouns, only **ein** is correct. This is a very important concept to learn! It is also reflected in the use of possessive adjectives such as **sein***(e)* (his) or **mein***(e)* *(my)*, which are also called 'ein-words'.

Gender is sometimes natural – **der Mann/ein Mann** (*man, masc.*), **die Frau/eine Frau** (woman, *fem.*), but more often it is not: **das Mädchen** (*girl, neutrum*). Nor does noun gender carry over from one language to another. The sun is feminine in German ***(die Sonne)*** but masculine in Spanish (***el sol***). A table is masculine in German ***(der Tisch)*** but feminine in French ***(la table)***. However, it is the word, not the thing that has gender, and it makes little sense to worry about the whys of gender. Just concentrate on learning the genders. Memorisation is key, but you can also use little hints to help you remember a noun's gender. For example, to remind yourself that **die Natur**, nature, is feminine, you might think of 'Mother Nature'. As you continue your studies, always learn a new noun and its gender together — as a unit. This important step will become increasingly important as you advance in German.

Substantive *Nouns*

NOMINATIVE SINGULAR

Article	Gender	Sample Nouns
der ein	**masc.**	der Bahnhof *(train station)*, Sohn *(son)*, Vater *(father)*, Wagen *(car)*, Zug *(draft, parade, train)*
die eine	**fem.**	die Anlage *(installation, park)*, Dame *(lady)*, Festung *(fortress)*, Gesundheit *(health)*, Luft *(air)*
das ein	**neut.**	das Boot *(boat)*, Dach *(roof)*, Geld *(money)*, Jahr *(year)*, Kino *(cinema, movie theater)*, Radio

NOMINATIVE PLURAL

Article	Gender	Sample Nouns (Plurals)
die keine meine	**plur.**	die Bücher *(books)*, Dächer *(roofs)*, die Fenster *(windows)*, Jahre *(years)*, Radios, Söhne *(sons)*, Zeitungen *(newspapers)*.

Note: All nouns, of any gender, become die in the plural. (Ein can't be plural, but other so-called ein-words can keine *[none]*, meine *[my]*, seine *[his]*, etc.) That is the good news. The bad news is that there are about sever ways to form the plural of German nouns, only one o which is to add an 's' - as in English.

Lesson 6

Two Important Verbs: haben and sein

To have and have not

Haben und nicht haben

The two most important German verbs are **haben** *(to have)* and **sein** *(to be)*. As in most languages, the verb 'to be' is one of the oldest verbs in German, and therefore one of the most irregular. The verb 'to have' is only slightly less irregular, but no less vital to surviving in German.

We will start with **haben**. Look at the following table for the conjugation of *haben (to have)* in the present tense, along with sample sentences. Notice the strong resemblance to English for many forms of this verb, with most forms only one letter off from the English (habe/have, hat/has). In the case of the familiar you (**du**), the German verb is identical to Old English: 'thou hast' = 'du hast'.

Haben is also used in some German expressions that are translated with 'to be' in English: *Ich habe Hunger.* = I'm hungry.

haben

Deutsch	**English**	**Sample Sentences**
SINGULAR		
ich habe	**I have**	Ich habe einen roten Wagen. *(...a red car.)*
du hast	**you (fam.) have**	Du hast mein Buch. *(...my book.)*
er hat	**he has**	Er hat ein blaues Auge. *(...a blue eye.)*
sie hat	**she has**	Sie hat blaue Augen. *(...blue eyes.)*
es hat	**it has**	Es hat keine Fehler. *(...no flaws.)*
PLURAL		
wir haben	**we have**	Wir haben keine Zeit. *(...no time.)*
ihr habt	**you (guys) have**	Habt ihr euer Geld? *(...your money?)*
sie haben	**they have**	Sie haben kein Geld. *(They have no money.)*
Sie haben	**you have**	*Haben Sie das Geld? (Do you have the money? Sie, formal 'you', is both singular and plural.)*

To be or not to be...
Sein oder nicht sein...

Look at the following table for the conjugation of **sein** (to be) in the present tense. Notice how similar the German and English forms are in the third person (ist/ is).

Sein

Deutsch	English	Sample Sentences
SINGULAR		
ich bin	**I am**	Ich bin. *(It's me.)*
du bist	**you (fam.) are**	Du bist mein Schatz. (...my darling/ treasure.)
er ist	**he is**	Er ist ein netter Kerl. (...a nice guy.)
sie ist	**she is**	Ist sie da? (Is she here?)
es ist	**it is**	Es ist mein Buch. (...my book.)
PLURAL		
wir sind	**we are**	'Wir sind das Volk!' ('We are the people/ nation!' - Slogan of 1989 East German protests in Leipzig.)
ihr seid	**you (guys) are**	Seid ihr unsere Freunde? (..our friends.)
sie sind	**they are**	Sie sind unsere Freunde. (..our friends.)
Sie sind	**you are**	Sind Sie Herr Meier? (Are you Mr. Meier? Sie, formal 'you', is both singular and plural.)

Lesson 7

German Verbs in the Present Tense

Unlike *haben* and *sein*, most German verbs follow a predictable pattern in the present tense. Once you learn the pattern for one German verb, you will know how most German verbs are conjugated. *(Yes, there are some irregular verbs that do not always follow the rules, but even they will usually have the same endings as other verbs.)*

The basics

Each verb has a basic 'infinitive' ('*to*') form. This is the form of the verb you find in a German dictionary. The verb 'to play' in English is the infinitive form. ('He plays' is a conjugated form.) The German equivalent of 'to play' is **spielen**. Each verb has a 'stem' form, the basic part of the verb left after you remove the **-en** ending. For **spielen** the stem is **spiel**- (**spielen** - **en**). To conjugate the verb—that is, to use it in a sentence—you must add the correct ending to the stem. If you want to say 'I play', you add an -**e** ending: 'ich spiel**e**' (*which can also be translated into English as 'I am playing'*). Each 'person' *(he, you, they, etc.)* requires its own ending on the verb. This is called 'conjugating the verb'. If you do not know how to conjugate verbs correctly, it means your German will sound strange to people who understand the language. German verbs require more different endings than English verbs. In English, we use only an **s** ending or no ending for most verbs: 'I/they/we/you play' or 'he/she plays'. In the present tense, German has a different ending for almost all of those verb situations: **ich spiele**, **sie spielen**, **du spielst**, **er spielt**, etc. Observe that the verb **spielen** has a different ending in each of the examples. If you want to sound intelligent in German, you need to learn when to use which ending. That's why we have this chart for you!

German has no present progressive tense ('am going'/'are buying'). The German Präsens 'ich kaufe' can be translated into English as 'I buy' or 'I am buying', depending on the context.

The chart below lists two sample German verbs—one an example of a 'normal' verb, the other an example of verbs that require a 'connecting e' in the 2nd person singular and plural, and the 3rd person singular (**du/ihr**, **er/sie/es**)—as in **er arbeitet**.

We have also included a helpful list of some representative common stem-changing verbs. These are verbs that follow the normal pattern of endings, but have a vowel change in their stem or base form (hence the name 'stem-changing'). In the subsequent chart, the verb endings for each pronoun *(person)* are indicated in **bold** type.

SPIELEN / TO PLAY

Deutsch	**English**	**Sample Sentence**
SINGULAR		
ich spiele	**I play**	Ich spiele gern Basketball.
du spielst	**you (fam.) play**	Spielst du Schach? *(chess)*
er spielt	**he plays**	Er spielt mit mir. *(with me)*
sie spielt	**she plays**	Sie spielt Karten. *(cards)*
es spielt	**it plays**	Es spielt keine Rolle. *It doesn't matter.*
PLURAL		
wir spielen	**we play**	Wir spielen Basketball.
ihr spielt	**you (guys) play**	Spielt ihr Monopoly?
sie spielen	**they play**	Sie spielen Golf.
Sie spielen	**you play**	Spielen Sie heute? *(**Sie**, formal 'you', is both singular and plural.)*

Now let's look at another German verb. This one is only slightly different from the others. The verb **arbeiten** (to work) belongs to a category of verbs that add a 'connecting' **e** in the 2nd person singular and plural, and the 3rd person singular (**du/ihr**, **er/sie/es**) in the present tense: **er arbeitet**. Verbs whose stem ends in **d** or **t** do this. The following are examples of verbs in this category: **antworten** *(to answer)*, **bedeuten** *(to mean)*, **enden** (to end), **senden** (to send). In the chart below, we have marked the 2nd and 3rd person conjugations with *.

ARBEITEN / TO WORK

Deutsch	**English**	**Sample Sentence**
SINGULAR		
ich arbeite	**I work**	Ich arbeite am Samstag.
du arbeitest *	**you (fam.) work**	Arbeitest du in der Stadt?
er arbeitet *	**he works**	Er arbeitet mit mir. (with me)
sie arbeitet *	**she works**	Sie arbeitet nicht.
es arbeitet *	**it works**	—
PLURAL		
wir arbeiten	**we work**	Wir arbeiten zu viel.
ihr arbeitet *	**you (guys) work**	Arbeitet ihr am Montag?
sie arbeiten	**they work**	Sie arbeiten bei BMW.
Sie arbeiten	**you work**	Arbeiten Sie heute? (**Sie**, formal 'you', is both singular and plural.)

Sample Stem-Changing Verbs

In the examples below, **er** stands for all three third-person pronouns (**er**, **sie**, **es**). Stem-changing verbs only change in the singular (except for **ich**). Their plural forms are completely regular.

Deutsch	**English**	**Sample Sentence**
Fahren	to travel	Er fährt nach Berlin.
er **fährt**	he travels	*He's travelling/going to Berlin.*
du **fährst**	you travel	Ich fahre nach Berlin.
		I'm travelling/going to Berlin.
Lesen	to read	Maria liest die Zeitung.
er **liest**	he reads	*Maria's reading the newspaper*
du **liest**	you read	Wir lesen die Zeitung.
		We read the newspaper.
Nehmen	to take	Karl nimmt sein Geld.
er **nimmt**	he takes	*Karl's taking his money.*
du **nimmst**	you take	Ich nehme mein Geld.
		I'm taking my money.
Vergessen	to forget	Er vergibt immer.
er **vergibt**	he forgets	*He always forgets.*
du **vergibt**	you forget	Vergib es! / Vergessen Sie es! Forget it!

Adjectives and Colours

Adjective Endings

German adjectives, like English ones, usually go in front of the noun they modify: 'der **gute** Mann' (the good man), 'das **große** Haus' (the big house/building), 'die **schöne** Dame' (the pretty lady). Unlike English adjectives, a German adjective in front of a noun has to have an ending *(-**e** in the examples above).* Just what that ending will be depends on several factors, including **gender** *(der, die, das)* and **case** *(nominative, accusative, dative).* But most of the time the ending is an -**e** or an -**en** *(in the plural).* With **ein**-words, the ending varies according to the modified noun's gender.

Look at the following table for the adjective endings in the nominative *(subject)* case:

With **definite article** *(der, die, das)* - **Nominative case**

Masculine	**Feminine**	**Neutrum**	**Plural**
der	**die**	**das**	**die**
Der neu**e** Wagen	die schön**e** Stadt	das alt**e** Auto	die neu**en** Bücher
the new car	the beautiful city	the old car	the new books

With **indefinite article** *(ein, kein, mein)* - **Nom. case**

Masculine	**Feminine**	**Neuter**	**Plural**
ein	**eine**	**ein**	**keine**
ein neu**er** neu**en** Bücher no new	eine schön**e** Wagen a new car city	ein alt**es** Stadt a beautiful	k e i n e Auto an old car books

Note that with **ein**-words, since the article may not tell us the gender of the following noun, the adjective ending often does this instead *(-**es** = **das**, -**er** = **der**).*

As in English, a German adjective can also come **after** the verb *(predicate adjective):* 'Das Haus ist groß'. *(The house is large.)* In such cases, the adjective will have NO ending.

Colours - Farben

The German words for colours usually function as adjectives and take the normal adjective endings. In certain situations, colours can also be nouns and are thus capitalised: 'eine Bluse in Blau' *(a blouse in blue);* 'das Blaue vom Himmel versprechen' *(to promise the moon lit., To promise the blue of the heaven).*

The chart below shows some of the more common colours with sample phrases.

Farbe	Colour	Colour Phrases with Adjective Endings
rot	**red**	der rote Wagen *(the red car)*, der Wagen ist rot
rosa	**pink**	die rosa Rosen *(the pink roses)*
blau	**blue**	ein blaues Auge *(a blue eye)*, er ist blau *(he's drunk)*
hell-blau	**light blue**	die hellblaue Bluse *(the light blue blouse)*
dunkel-blau	**dark blue**	die dunkelblaue Bluse *(the dark blue blouse)*
grün	**green**	der grün Hut *(the green hat)*
gelb	**yellow**	die gelben Seiten *(the yellow pages)*, ein gelbes Auto
weiß	**white**	das weiße Papier *(the white paper)*
schwarz	**black**	der schwarze Koffer *(the black suitcase)*

Land und Leute kennenlernen

Getting to know the country and the people

Drei Personen

Let us look at three imaginary people from three different German-speaking countries. We'll find out where they live (**wohnen**), what nationality they are, and the language they speak (**sprechen**).

KARL Karl wohnt in Berlin. Er ist Deutscher. Er spricht Deutsch.
Karl lives in Berlin. He's German. He speaks German.

INGE Inge wohnt in Graz. Sie ist Österreicherin. Sie spricht Deutsch.
Inge lives in Graz. She's Austrian. She speaks German.

MARTIN Martin wohnt in Genf. Er ist Schweizer. Er spricht Französisch und Deutsch.
Martin lives in Geneva. He's Swiss. He speaks French and German.

If we want to get this information from the three people, here is what we would ask (**fragen**) in German and what they would answer (**antworten**):

KARL Wo wohnen Sie? - Ich wohne in Berlin.
Welche Nationalität haben Sie? - Ich bin Deutscher.
Welche Sprache sprechen Sie? - Ich spreche Deutsch.

INGE Wo wohnen Sie? - Ich wohne in Graz.
Welche Nationalität haben Sie? - Ich bin Österreicherin.
Welche Sprache sprechen Sie? - Ich spreche Deutsch.

MARTIN Wo wohnen Sie? - Ich wohne in Genf.
Welche Nationalität haben Sie? - Ich bin Schweizer.
Welche Sprache sprechen Sie? - Ich spreche Französisch und Deutsch.

YOU Wo wohnen Sie? - Ich wohne in ____.
Welche Nationalität haben Sie?
- Ich bin Amerikaner/Amerikanerin.
- Ich bin Australier/Australierin.
- Ich bin Engländer/Engländerin.
Welche Sprache sprechen Sie?
- Ich spreche Englisch.

Most countries are neuter (***das***) in German, but do not use the article in most cases: **in Deutschland** (*in Germany*), **nach Deutschland** (*to Germany*). Some nations, such as **die Schweiz** (*Switzerland*) and **die Türkei** (*Turkey*), are feminine and a few are plural (***die Vereinigten Staaten***, *USA*). A very few, mostly Islamic countries, are masculine: **der Irak**, **der Iran**.

Now you can try out what you have learned. Here are two exercises (***Übungen***) to practice talking about where you live, nationality and language. After you complete each exercise, you can check your answers in the answer keys provided.

Exercise

1. How would you answer the same questions for yourself? Model your answers on those shown above.

1. Wo wohnen Sie? - Ich ____________________

2. Welche Nationalität haben Sie? - ____________

3. Welche Sprache sprechen Sie? - ____________

Answers

1. Wo wohnen Sie?

ANTWORT (answer): Ich wohne in Chicago/London/Los Angeles. (*your city/town*)
PRONUNCIATION: (*ich voh - nuh in...)*

2. Welche Nationalität haben Sie?

ANTWORT: Ich bin Amerikaner(*in*)/Engländer(in)/ Kanadier(in). (your nationality) PRONUNCIATION: (ich bin...)

Note: Do not use 'ein' or 'eine' in your answer. Females should answer with the fem. -**in** form (*i.e.*, ***Engländerin*** or ***Amerikanerin***).

3. Welche Sprache sprechen Sie?

ANTWORT: **Ich spreche Englisch (Französisch, Spanisch)**. PRONUNCIATION: (*ich shprech - uh...*)

2. Identify the country and nationality of these 10 famous people. Note: 'kommt aus' means 'comes from'.

Wer hat welche Nationalität?

1. Arnold Schwarzenegger kommt aus _____. Er ist _____.

2. Steffi Graf (*Tennis*) kommt aus _____. Sie ist _____.

3. Tom Cruise...

4. Prinz Charles...

5. Julia Roberts...

6. Wladimir Putin...

7. Mel Gibson...

8. Alex Trebek ('*Jeopardy*') ...

9. Catherine Deneuve...

10. Sean Connery...

Answers

1. Arnold Schwarzenegger kommt aus **Österreich**. Er ist **Österreicher**. (*ay*ster-RYCH-er*)

2. Steffi Graf kommt aus **Deutschland**. Sie ist **Deutsche**. (DOYT-shuh)

3. Tom Cruise kommt aus **den USA** (aus den Vereinigten Staaten). Er ist **Amerikaner**.

4. Prinz Charles kommt aus **England**. Er ist **Engländer**.
- or
...aus **Großbritannien**. Er ist **Brite**.

5. Julia Roberts kommt aus **den USA** (aus den Vereinigten Staaten). Sie ist **Amerikanerin**.

6. Wladimir (Vladimir) Putin kommt aus **Rubland**. Er ist **Russe**. (ROOSUH)

7. Mel Gibson kommt aus **Australien**. Er ist **Australier**. (ow-STRAHL-yer)

8. Alex Trebek ('Jeopardy') kommt aus **Kanada**. Er ist **Kanadier**.

9. Catherine Deneuve kommt aus **Frankreich**. Sie ist **Französin**. (frahn-TSAY**-zin)

10. Sean Connery kommt aus **Schottland**. Er ist **Schotte**. (SHOT-uh)

* Pronounce while rounding lips.

** While pronouncing AY, round your lips.

Lesson 8

Other Countries and their Languages

Here are some other countries and languages.

LAND	COUNTRY	SPRACHE
Belgien *(B)*	Belgium	Französisch French
	Flämisch	
Flemish		
Dänemark *(DK)*	Denmark Danish	Dänisch
Finnland *(FIN)*	Finland Finnish	Finnisch
Griechenland *(GR)*	Greece	Griechisch Greek
Kenia *(EAK)*	Kenya	Suaheli/Kisuaheli Swahili Englisch English

Kuba *(C)*	Cuba Spanish	Spanisch
die Türkei (*TR*)	Turkey Turkish	Türkisch

Now look at these sample sentences for several countries. Notice how we say 'in' a country, as well as the German terms for nationalities and languages.

LAND - SPRACHE
Country - Language

Kuba	Die Kubaner sprechen Spanisch. In Kuba spricht man Spanisch. *The Cubans speak Spanish. In Cuba they speak Spanish.*
Türkei	Die Türken sprechen Türkisch. In der Türkei spricht man Türkisch. *The Turks speak Turkish. In Turkey they speak Turkish.*
Belgien	Die Belgier sprechen Flämisch oder Französisch. In Belgien spricht man Flämisch oder Französisch. *The Belgians speak Flemish or French. In Belgium they speak Flemish or French.*

Lesson 9

Numbers and Counting

The numbers and counting in German are not difficult to learn, but... true mastery of numbers, in any language, takes time. It is easy to learn to rattle off the numbers - 'eins, zwei, drei'... and so forth.

However, most of the time numbers are used in more practical ways: in telephone numbers, in math problems, in prices, for addresses, etc. Also, because you have already internalised the numbers in English or another first language, there can be the same kind of interference that happens with other vocabulary.

So, do learn to say the numbers, but also try our exercises to see if you really know how to deal with them.

If someone tells you a phone number in German, can you write it down?

Can you do simple addition or subtraction in German?

DIE ZAHLEN 0-10

0 **null**

1 **eins**

2 **zwei** *

3 **drei**

4 **vier**

5 **fünf**

6 **sechs**

7 **sieben**

8 **acht**

9 **neun**

10 **zehn**

* Often zwo is used to avoid confusion with drei.

DIE ZAHLEN 11-20

11 **elf**

12 **zwölf**

13 **dreizehn**

14 **vierzehn**

15 **fünfzehn**

16 **sechzehn**

17 **siebzehn**

18 **achtzehn**

19 **neunzehn**

20 **zwanzig**

Exercise

1. Write out the answer to the following math problems in German.

1. **zwei + fünf =** ______________
2. **zwölf - zwei =** ______________
3. **drei + neun =** ______________
4. **vier - vier =** ______________
5. **eins + sechs =** ______________
6. **dreizehn - zwei =** ______________
7. **sieben + elf =** ______________

1. **zwei + fünf = sieben** (2 + 5 = 7)
2. **zwölf - zwei = zehn** (12 - 2 = 10)
3. **drei + neun = zwölf** (3 + 9 = 12)

4. **vier - vier = null** (4 - 4 = 0)

5. **eins + sechs = sieben** (1 + 6 = 7)

6. **dreizehn - zwei = elf** (13 - 2 = 11)

7. **sieben + elf = achtzehn** (7 + 11 = 18)

2. Diktat (Dictation) - Write out the following phone numbers as numerals.

1. **null, zwo; zwölf, elf, zwanzig =** ____________

2. **neunzehn; null, fünf; sechzehn, =** ____________

3. **null, acht; zwölf, elf, zwanzig =** ____________

4. **null, drei; vier, sieben; achtzehn, zwanzig =** ____

5. **dreizehn, zwölf, zehn, vierzehn =** ____________

1. **null, zwo; zwölf, elf, zwanzig = 02 12 11 20**

2. **neunzehn; null, fünf; sechzehn = 19 05 16**

3. **null, acht; zwölf, elf, zwanzig = 08 12 11 20**

4. **null, drei; vier, sieben; achtzehn, zwanzig = 03 47 18 20**

5. **dreizehn, zwölf, zehn, vierzehn = 13 12 10 14**

Die Zahlen und zählen (21-100)

In the previous page, we introduced you to the German numbers from 0 to 20. Now it is time to expand to 'higher' math — from 21 (***einundzwanzig***) to 100 (***hundert***). Once you have a grasp of the twenties, the rest of the numbers up to 100 and beyond are similar and easy to learn. You will also be using many of the numbers you learned from zero (***null***) to 20.

For the German numbers above 20, think of the English nursery rhyme 'Sing a Song of Sixpence' and the line 'four and twenty blackbirds' ('baked in a pie'). In German you say one-and-twenty (***einundzwanzig***) rather than twenty-one. All of the numbers over 20 work the same way: **zweiundzwanzig** (*22*), **einundreißig** (*31*), **dreiundvierzig** (*43*), etc. No matter how long they may be, German numbers are written as one word.

For numbers above (***ein***)**hundert**, the pattern just repeats itself. The number 125 is **hundertfünfundzwanzig**. To say 215 in German, you simply put **zwei** in front of **hundert** to make **zweihundertfünfzehn**. Three hundred is **dreihundert** and so on.

Wie viel? / Wie viele?

To ask 'how much' you say **wie viel**. To ask 'how many' you say **wie viele**. For example, a simple math problem would be: **Wie viel ist drei und vier?** *(How much is three and four?)*. To ask 'how many cars' you would say: **Wie viele Autos?** as in **Wie viele Autos hat Karl?** *(How many cars does Karl have?)*.

After you go over the number charts below... If you hear a number above 20 in German, can you write it down? Can you do simple math in German?

Die Zahlen 20-100 (by tens)

20 **zwanzig**
30 **dreißig**
40 **vierzig**
50 **fünfzig**
60 **sechzig**
70 **siebzig**
80 **achtzig**
90 **neunzig**
100 **hundert** *
* *or* einhundert

Note: The number **sechzig** (60) drops the **s** in **sechs**. The number **siebzig** (70) drops the **en** in **sieben**. The number **dreißig** (30) is the only one of the tens that doesn't end with **-zig**. (**dreißig = dreissig**)

Die Zahlen 21-30

21 **einundzwanzig**
22 **zweiundzwanzig**
23 **dreiundzwanzig**
24 **vierundzwanzig**
25 **fünfundzwanzig**
26 **sechsundzwanzig**
27 **siebenundzwanzig**
28 **achtundzwanzig**
29 **neunundzwanzig**
30 **dreißig**

Note: The number **dreißig** *(30)* is the only one of the tens that doesn't end with **-zig**.

Die Zahlen 31-40

31 **einunddreißig**
32 **zweiunddreißig**
33 **dreiunddreißig**
34 **vierunddreißig**
35 **fünfunddreißig**
36 **sechsunddreißig**
37 **siebenunddreißig**
38 **achtunddreißig**
39 **neununddreißig**
40 **vierzig**

Die Zahlen 41-100 (selected numbers)

41 **einundvierzig**
42 **zweiundvierzig**
53 **dreiundfünfzig**
64 **vierundsechzig**
75 **fünfundsiebzig**
86 **sechsundachtzig**
87 **siebenundachtzig**
98 **achtundneunzig**
99 **neunundneunzig**
100 **hundert**

Einleitung

For each number, two forms are shown: *(1)* the **cardinal** number *(Kardinalzahl - 1, 2, 3...)* and *(2)* **ordinal** number (*Ordinalzahl* - 1st, 2nd, 3rd...). In some cases the **fractional** number *(Bruchzahl - 1/2, 1/5, 1/100...)* is also given. (To make fractions [*Brüche*], just add -**tel** or -**el** to the number: **acht + el = achtel** [an eighth], **zehn + tel = zehntel** [a tenth].) Although the masculine (i.e., calendar date) form is shown for the ordinal numbers, they can also be feminine ***(die)***, neuter ***(das)*** or plural, depending on the noun they are used with: **das erste Auto**, **die zweite Tür**, **die ersten Menschen**, etc.

0 **null** *(zero, nought)*

For decimal numbers ***(Dezimalzahlen)***, German uses a comma ***(das Komma)*** where English uses a decimal point: 0.638 *(English)* = 0,638 *(spoken: 'null Komma sechs drei acht')* or 1.08 *(English)* = 1,08 *(spoken: 'eins Komma null acht')*.

1 **eins** - **der erste**, **der 1.** *(first)*

one o'clock **ein Uhr** *(time, no ending on 'ein')*
one/a clock **eine Uhr** *(article, -e ending on 'ein')*
(date) on the first **am ersten**
on 1 May, on May first, the first of May **am ersten Mai**, **am 1. Mai**

2 **zwei** - **der zweite**, **der 2.** *(second)* - **halb, die Hälfte** *(half, one-half)*

Often the alternative form **zwo** is used to avoid confusion with **drei**.

3 **drei** - **der dritte**, **der 3.** *(third)* - **drittel** *(one-third)*

4 **vier** - **der vierte** *(fourth)* - **viertel-**, **das Viertel** *(one-fourth, quarter)*

5 **fünf** - **der fünfte** *(fifth)*

6 **sechs** - **der sechste** *(sixth)*

7 **sieben** - **der siebte** *(seventh)*

8 **acht** - **der achte** *(eighth)*

9 **neun** - **der neunte** *(ninth)*

10 **zehn** - **der zehnte**, **der 10.** *(tenth)*

11 **elf** - **der elfte**, **der 11.** *(eleventh)*

12 **zwölf** - **der zwölfte**, **der 12.** (twelfth)

13 **dreizehn** - **der dreizehnte** (thirteenth), **am dreizehnten**

14 **vierzehn** - **der vierzehnte** (fourteenth) - **am vierzehnten**

15 **fünfzehn** - **der fünfzehnte** (fifteenth) - **am fünfzehnten**

16 **sechzehn** - **der sechzehnte** (sixteenth)

17 **siebzehn** - **der siebzehnte** (seventeenth)

18 **achtzehn** - **der achtzehnte** (eighteenth)

19 **neunzehn** - **der neunzehnte** (nineteenth)

20 **zwanzig** - **der zwanzigste**, **der 20.** (the twentieth, 20th) - **am zwanzigsten Juni**, **am 20. Juni** (on the 20th of June)

To say 'in the twenties (the '20s)' - short for 'the 1920s' - in German you say '**in den zwangziger Jahren**'. The same method is used for all the other decades ('30s, '40s, etc.) except for the 1900s and the tens.

21 **einundzwanzig** - **der einundzwanzigste**, **der 21.** (the twenty-first, 21st) - **am einundzwanzigsten Juni**, **am 21. Juni** (on the 21st of June)

22 **zweiundzwanzig** - **der zweiundzwanzigste**, **der 22.** (the twenty-second, 22nd)

23 **dreiundzwanzig** - **der dreiundzwanzigste**, **der 23.** (the twenty-third, 23rd)

24 **vierundzwanzig** - **der vierundzwanzigste**, **der 24.** (the twenty-fourth, 24th)

25 **fünfundzwanzig** - **der fünfundzwanzigste**, **der 25.** (the twenty-fifth, 25th)

26 **sechsundzwanzig** - **der sechsundzwanzigste**, **der**

26. (the twenty-sixth, 26th)

27 **siebenundzwanzig** - **der siebenundzwanzigste**, **der 27.** (the twenty-seventh, 27th)

28 **achtundzwanzig** - **der achtundzwanzigste**, **der 28.** (the twenty-eighth, 28th)

29 **neunundzwanzig** - **der neunfundzwanzigste**, **der 29.** (the twenty-ninth, 29th)

30 **dreißig** - **der dreißigste**, **der 30.** (the thirtieth, 30th)

Note that, unlike the other tens (20, 40, 50, etc.), **dreißig** has no 'z' in its spelling.

31 **einunddreißig** - **der einunddreißigste**, **der 31.** (the thirty-first, 31st)

32 **zweiunddreißig** - **der zweiunddreißigste**, **der 32.** (the thirty-second, 32nd)

33 **dreiunddreißig** - **der dreiunddreißigste**, **der 33.** (the thirty-third, 33rd)

(Continues as with the 20s)

40 **vierzig** - **der vierzigste**, **der 40.** (the fortieth, 40th)

41 **einundvierzig** - **der einundvierzigste**, **der 41.** (the forty-first, 41st)

42 **zweiundvierzig** - **der zweiundvierzigste**, **der 42.** (the forty-second, 42nd)

43 **dreiundvierzig** - **der dreiundvierzigste**, **der 43.** (the forty-third, 43rd)

(Continues as with the previous 20s, 30s, etc.)

50 **fünfzig – der fünfzigste, der 50,** *(the fiftieth, 50th)*

51 **einundfünfzig – der einundfünfzigste, der 51.** *(the fifty-first, 51st)*

52 **zweiundfünfzig – der zweiundfünfzigste, der 52.** *(the fifty-second, 52nd*

53 **dreiundfünfzig – der dreiundfünfzigste, der 53.** *(the fifty-third, 53rd)*

(54, 55... continues as with the previous 30s, 40s, etc.)

Some Math Terms :

To add **addieren**

algebra **e algebra**

calculus **s Differentialrechnung, e Integralrechnung**

to divide **dividieren**

divided by **getitt durch**

equals **ist gleichts**

equation **e Formel**

geometry **e Geometrie**

minus, less **minus** *(MEE-noos)*, **weniger** *(VAYN-i-guhr)*

to multiply **multiplizieren**

plus, and **plus** *(PLOOS)*, ***und***

to subtract **subtrahieren**

times *(2 3=6)* **mal *(2 mal 3 = 6)***

trigonometry **e Trigonometrie**

Note : 'e' denotes definite article 'die'

Lesson 10

The Calendar and Appointments: Days, Months, Dative Phrases and Seasons

After studying this chapter, you'll be able to: *(1)* say the days and months in German, *(2)* express calendar dates, *(3)* talk about the seasons and *(4)* talk about dates and deadlines ***(Termine)*** in German. We'll also review some of the vocabulary for time and telling time that you learned in earlier chapters.

Luckily, because they are based on Latin, the English and German words for the months are almost identical. The days in many cases are also similar because of a common Germanic heritage. Most of the days bear the names of Teutonic gods in both languages. For example, the Germanic god of war and thunder, Thor, lends his name to both English **Thursday** and German **Donnerstag** *(thunder =* ***Donner****)*.

Let's start with the days of the week ***(Tage der Woche)***. Most of the days in German end in the word ***(der)*** **Tag**, just as the English days end in 'day'. The German week (and calendar) starts with Monday ***(Montag)*** rather than Sunday. Each day is shown with its common two-letter abbreviation.

Tage der Woche
Days of the Week

DEUTSCH	**ENGLISH**
Montag *(Mo)* *(Mond-Tag)*	Monday 'moon day'
Dienstag *(Di)*	Tuesday
Mittwoch *(Mi)* *(mid-week)*	Wednesday *(Wednes day)*
Donnerstag *(Do)* 'thunder-day'	Thursday *(Thur's day)*
Freitag *(Fr)* *(Fry-Tag)*	Friday *(Freya's day)*
Samstag *(Sa)* Sonnabend *(Sa)* *(used in North Germany)*	 Saturday *(Saturn's day)*
Sonntag *(So)* *(Sonne-Tag)*	Sunday 'sun day'

The seven days of the week are of masculine gender ***(der)*** since they usually end in -**tag**. *(The two exceptions, **Mittwoch** and **Sonnabend**, are also masculine.)* Note that there are two words for Saturday. **Samstag** is used in most of Germany, in Austria and in German Switzerland. **Sonnabend** *('Sunday eve')* is used in eastern Germany and roughly north of the city of Münster in northern Germany. So, in Hamburg, Rostock, Leipzig or Berlin, it's **Sonnabend**; in Cologne, Frankfurt, Munich or Vienna 'Saturday' is **Samstag**. Both words for 'Saturday' are understood all over the German-speaking world, but you should try to use the one most common in the region you're in. Note the two-letter abbreviation for each of the days *(**Mo**, **Di**, **Mi**, etc.)*. These are used on calendars, schedules and German/Swiss watches that indicate the day and date.

To say 'on Monday' or 'on Friday' you use the prepositional phrase **am Montag** or **am Freitag**. *(The word **am** is actually a contraction of **an** and **dem**, the dative form of **der**. We'll explain more about that below.)* Here are some commonly used phrases for the days of the week:

Day Phrases

English	**Deutsch**
on Monday *(on Tuesday, Wednesday, etc.)*	am Montag *(am Dienstag, Mittwoch, usw.)*
(on) Mondays *(on Tuesdays, Wednesdays, etc.)*	montags *(dienstags, mittwochs, usw.)*
every Monday, Mondays	jeden Montag/ Moutags
(every Tuesday, Wednesday, etc.) Mittwoch, usw.)	*(jeden Dienstag,*
this Tuesday	*(am)* kommenden Dienstag
last Wednesday	letzten Mittwoch
the Thursday after next	übernächsten Donnerstag
every other Friday	jeden zweiten Freitag
Today is Tuesday.	Heute ist Dienstag.

Tomorrow is Wednesday.	Morgen ist Mittwoch.
Yesterday was Monday.	Gestern war Montag.

A few words about the DATIVE case. In another chapter, we will look at the **accusative** *(direct object)* case. Below is a chart of what happens to the articles ***(der, die, das)*** in the three main cases.

The **dative** case is used as the object of certain prepositions *(as with dates)* and as the indirect object of a verb. Here we are concentrating on the use of the accusative and dative in expressing dates. Here is a chart of those changes. *(Items in the darker boxes do not change.)*

NOMINATIV-AKKUSATIV-DATIV

GENDER	**Nominativ**	**Akkusativ**	**Dativ**
MASC.	der/jeder	den/jeden	dem
NEUT.	das	das	dem
FEM.	die	die	der

Examples: am Dienstag *(on Tuesday, dative)*, jeden Tag *(every day, accusative)*

Note: The masculine *(der)* and neuter *(das)* make the same changes *(look the same)* in the DATIV case. Adjectives or numbers used in the dative will have an -en ending: am sechsten April.

Now we want to apply the information in the chart above. When we use the prepositions **an** (on) and **in** (in) with days, months or dates, they take the dative case. Days and months are masculine, so we end up with a combination of **an** or **in** plus **dem**, which equals **am** or **im**. Additionally, some date expressions that do not use prepositions ***(jeden Dienstag, letzten Mittwoch)*** are in the accusative case.

A. TAGE - Abkürzungen

Write out the full word for each of the following German abbreviations ***(Abkürzungen)*** for the days of the week. Then also write out the English word for that day.

1. **Sa** ________________ = (Engl.) ______________
2. **Do** ________________ = ________________
3. **Fr** ________________ = ________________
4. **So** ________________ = ________________
5. **Mi** ________________ = ________________
6. **Mo** ________________ = ________________
7. **Di** ________________ = ________________

Answers

1. **Sa Samstag** = (Engl.) **Saturday** *AND*
   Sa Sonnabend = **Saturday**
2. **Do Donnerstag** = **Thursday**
3. **Fr Freitag** = **Friday**
4. **So Sonntag** = **Sunday**
5. **Mi Mittwoch** = **Wednesday**
6. **Mo Montag** = **Monday**
7. **Di Dienstag** = **Tuesday**

B. WANN? An welchem Tag?

Write a complete sentence in German that says the same thing as the English.

Beispiel: They're coming on Wednesday. - **Sie kommen am Mittwoch**.

8. Is he coming on Monday or (**oder**) Tuesday? -

9. The meeting (**das Treffen**) is this Friday. -

10. Tomorrow is Saturday. -

11. Yesterday was Thursday. -

12. Wasn't that last Monday? -

Answers

8. Is he coming on Monday or (**oder**) Tuesday? - **Kommt er am Montag oder am Dienstag?**

9. The meeting (**das Treffen**) is this Friday. - **Das Treffen ist (am) kommenden Freitag**.

10. Tomorrow is Saturday. - **Morgen ist Samstag/ Sonnabend**.

11. Yesterday was Thursday. - **Gestern war Donnerstag**.

12. Wasn't that last Monday? - **War das nicht letzten Montag?**

C. Tagesrätsel

Items 13-15 are a series of easy word puzzles. Write in the missing day of the week for each item.

13. Heute ist Donnerstag. Morgen ist ____________ .

14. Gestern war Sonnabend. Heute ist ____________ .

15. Heute ist Montag. Übermorgen ist ____________ .

Answers

13. Heute ist Donnerstag. Morgen ist **Freitag**.

14. Gestern war Sonnabend. Heute ist **Sonntag**.

15. Heute ist Montag. Übermorgen ist **Mittwoch**.

In this section, we look at the months, the seasons, and how to say a calendar date in German. In the list of months below, you can see that the English and German are either close or identical, but note the pronunciation shown for some of the months.

Die Monate - The Months

DEUTSCH	**ENGLISH**
Januar YAHN-oo-ahr	January
Februar	February
März MEHRTS	March
April	April
Mai MYE	May
Juni	June
Juli	July
August ow-GOOST	August
September	September
Oktober	October
November	November
Dezember	December

The months are all of masculine gender ***(der)***. There are two words used for July. **Juli** *(YOO-LEE)* is the standard form, but German-speakers often say **Julei** *(YOO-LYE)* to avoid confusion with **Juni** – in much the same way that **zwo** is used for **zwei**.

Before we talk more about the months, let's also look at the four seasons, **die vier Jahreszeiten**.

Die Jahreszeiten - The Seasons

Jahreszeit	**Monate**
der Frühling das Frühjahr *(Adj.)* frühlingshaft	März, April, Mai im Frühling - in the spring
der Sommer *(Adj.)* sommerlich	Juni, Juli, August im Sommer - in the summer
der Herbst *(Adj.)* herbstlich	Sept., Okt., Nov. im Herbst - in the fall/ autumn
der Winter *(Adj.)* winterlich	Dez., Jan., Feb. im Winter - in the winter

The seasons are all masculine gender *(except for **das Frühjahr**, another word for spring)*. The months for each season above are, of course, for the northern hemisphere where Germany and the other German-speaking countries lie.

When speaking of a season in general *('Autumn is my favorite season'.)*, in German you almost always use the article: '**Der Herbst ist meine Lieblingsjahreszeit'.** The adjectival forms shown above translate as 'springlike, springy', 'summerlike' or 'autumnal, falllike' (**sommerliche Temperaturen** = 'summerlike/summery temperatures'). In some cases, the noun form is used as a prefix, as in **die Winterkleidung** = 'winter clothing' or **die Sommermonate** = 'the summer months'. The prepositional phrase **im *(in dem)*** is used for all the seasons when you want to say, for instance, 'in *(the)* spring' ***(im Frühling)***. This is the same as for the months.

More on the months

To say 'in May' or 'in November' you use the prepositional phrase **im Mai** or **im November**. *(The word* ***im*** *is a contraction of* ***in*** *and* ***dem****, the dative form of* ***der****.)* To give a date, such as 'on July 4th', you use **am** *(as with the days)* and the ordinal number *(4th, 5th)*: **am vierten Juli**, usually written **am 4. Juli**. The period after the number represents the -**ten** ending on the number and is the same as the -th, -rd, or -nd ending used for English ordinal numbers.

Note that numbered dates in German *(and in all of the European languages)* are always written in the order of day, month, year - rather than month, day, year. For example, in German the date 1/6/01 would be written 6.1.01 *(which is Epiphany or Three Kings, the 6th of January 2001)*. This is the logical order, moving from the smallest unit *(the day)* to the largest *(the year)*. Here are some commonly used phrases for the months and calendar dates:

Calendar Date Phrases

English	**Deutsch**
in August *(in June, October, etc.)*	im August *(im Juni, Oktober, usw.)*
on June 14th *(spoken)*	am vierzehnten Juni
on June 14, 2001 *(written)* 14.6.01	am 14. Juni 2001 -
on the first of May *(spoken)*	am ersten Mai
on May 1, 2001 *(written)*	am 1. Mai 2001 - 1.5.01

The ordinal numbers are so-called because they express the order in a series, in this case for dates. But the same principle applies to the 'first door' ***(die erste Tür)*** or the 'fifth element' ***(das fünfte Element)***.

In most cases, the ordinal number is the cardinal number with a -**te** or -**ten** ending. Just as in English, some German numbers have irregular ordinals: one/first ***(eins/erste)*** or three/third ***(drei/dritte)***. Below is a sainple chart with ordinal numbers that would be required for dates.

Sample Ordinal Numbers (Dates)

English	**Deutsch**
1 the first - on the first/1st	der erste - am ersten/1.
2 the second - on the second/2nd	der zweite - am zweiten/2.
3 the third - on the third/3rd	der dritte - am dritten/3.
4 the fourth - on the fourth/4th	der vierte - am vierten/4.
5 the fifth - on the fifth/5th	der fünfte - am fünften/5.
6 the sixth - on the sixth/6th	der sechste - am sechsten/6.
11 the eleventh on the eleventh/11th	der elfte - am elften/11.
21 the twenty-first on the twenty-first/21st	der einundzwanzigste am einundzwanzigsten/21.
31 the thirty-first on the thirty-first/31st	der einunddreißigste am einunddreißigsten/31.

Exercise

A. Jahreszeiten und Monate

Write out the three months *(in German)* for each of the seasons.

(In the northern hemisphere.)

1. **Herbst**: ___________________

2. **Sommer**: ___________________

3. **Frühling**: ___________________

4. **Winter**: ___________________

Answers

1. **Herbst**: **September Oktober November**

2. **Sommer**: **Juni Juli August**

3. **Frühling**: **März April Mai**

4. **Winter**: **Dezember Januar Februar**

B. Wann ist der Feiertag?

Write a sentence giving the date in German for the following holidays or celebrations. Follow the example.

Beispiel: **Weihnachten** *(Christmas)*: **Weihnachten ist am 25. Dezember - am fünfundzwanzigsten Dez..**

5. **Halloween**:

6. **Heilige Drei Könige** *(Epiphany, Three Kings)*:

7. **Unabhängigkeitstag** *(Independence Day)* **in den USA**:

8. **Tag der deutschen Einheit** *(German Unity Day)*:

9. **Allerheiligen** *(All Saints' Day)*:

10. **Nikolaustag** *(St. Nicholas' Day)*:

Answers

5. **Halloween**: **Halloween ist am 31. Oktober - am einunddreißigsten Okt.**

6. **Heilige Drei Könige** *(Epiphany, Three Kings)*: **Heilige Drei Könige ist am 6. Januar - am sechsten Jan.**

7. **Unabhängigkeitstag** *(Independence Day)* **in den USA**: **Unabhängigkeitstag ist am 4. Juli - am vierten Juli**

8. **Tag der deutschen Einheit** *(German Unity Day)*: **Der Tag der deutschen Einheit ist am 3. Oktober - am dritten Okt.**

9. **Allerheiligen** *(All Saints' Day)*: **Allerheiligen ist am 1. November - am ersten Nov.**

10. **Nikolaustag** *(St. Nicholas' Day)*: **Nikolaustag ist am 6. Dezember - am sechsten Dez.**

C. Fragen

Items 11-15 are German questions about dates and events. Write a logical answer in German.

11. In welchem Monat ist Weihnachten?

12. Wie schreibt man das Datum 'Dec. 7, 1941' in Zahlen auf Deutsch?

13. Wann feiert man 'Thanksgiving' in Kanada?

14. Wie schreibt oder sagt man das deutsche Datum '7.8.04' auf Englisch?

15. Wann gehen Sie meistens auf Urlaub? *(go on vacation/ holidays)*

Answers

11. In welchem Monat ist Weihnachten?

Weihnachten ist im Dezember.

12. Wie schreibt man das Datum 'Dec. 7, 1941' in Zahlen auf Deutsch?

Man schreibt: 7.12.1941 (der 7. Dez. 1941).

13. Wann feiert man 'Thanksgiving' in Kanada?
In Kanada feiert man Thanksgiving am zweiten Montag im Oktober.

14. Wie schreibt oder sagt man das deutsche Datum '7.8.04' auf Englisch?

Man sagt oder schreibt: the seventh of August 2004 (Aug. 7, 2004).

15. Wann gehen Sie meistens auf Urlaub? (go on vacation/holidays)

Ich gehe meistens im Sommer/im Juni/im August auf Urlaub.

Lesson 11

Common Greetings and Courtesies

Below you will find some of the most common German greetings (***Grüße***) and pleasantries (***Nettigkeiten***). Be aware that German, more than English, makes a clear distinction between formal (***Sie***) and familiar (*first name, **du***) forms of expression. Phrases marked 'familiar' or 'casual' should only be used in informal, first-name situations. Germans tend to be more formal and use first names only in certain situations.

German Greetings and Courtesies

Deutsch	**English**
- Hallo!	Hello! - Hi!
Grüß Gott!	Hello! *(southern Germany and Austria)*
Grüβ dich! Greetings!! (Hi!!)	Grüβ dich is Greetings (Hi) not Hello.

Guten Morgen! - Morgen!	Good morning!-Morning!
Guten Abend!	Good evening!
Gute Nacht!	Good night!
Wie geht es Ihnen?	How are you?
Wie geht's?	How are you? *(familiar, informal)*
Danke, gut.	Fine, thanks.
Sehr gut.	Very fine
Es geht.	Okay. So-so.
Nicht so gut.	Not so well.
Auf Wiedersehen.	See you later.
Tschüs! (*casual*)	Good Bye.

Requests - Bitten

Was möchten Sie?	What would you like?
Ich möchte...	I would like...
Darf ich?	May I?
Können Sie mir helfen?	Can you help me?
Ja/Nein - Danke! - Bitte Schön	Yes/No - Thanks - You're Welcome
Bitte! - Ja, bitte!	Please! - Yes, please!
Danke!	Thanks! - No thanks!
Danke schön!	Thank you very much!
Vielen Dank!	Thanks a lot! - Many thanks!
Bitte schön!	You're welcome!
Nein, danke!	No thanks!

Lesson 12

Terms Related to Family and Yourself

In this chapter we introduce vocabulary and grammar related to talking about your family and yourself. You'll learn words and phrases that will let you talk about your own family in German, as well as understand what someone else says about his or her family. You can also listen to the vocabulary!

In addition to the members of a family ***(die Familie**, dee fah-Meelee-uh)*, you'll learn how to ask someone's name *(and answer)*, talk about family relationships and give the ages of people. We will also discuss the difference between the formal and informal 'you' in German — a vital cultural and language distinction that English-speakers need to understand!

Cognates

One of the first things you'll notice is that many of the German words for the family are similar to the English terms. It is easy to see the close Germanic language 'family resemblance' between *brother*/**Bruder**, *father/*

Vater, or *daughter*/**Tochter**. We call these similar words in two languages **cognates**. There are a lot of English-German cognates for the family. Others are familiar because of common Latin or French origins: *family*/**Familie**, *uncle*/**Onkel**, etc.

After you have studied this chapter, you will be able to read and understand a short paragraph in German about your or someone else's family. You'll even be able to draw your own family tree ***(Stammbaum)*** in German!

Familienmitglieder - Family Members

Notice in the phrases below that when you talk about a feminine *(die)* person *(or thing)*, the possessive pronoun mein ends in e. When talking about a masculine *(der)* person *(or thing)*, mein has no ending in the nominative (subject) case. Other possessive forms *(sein, his; dein, your, etc.)* work the same way. The final e in German is always pronounced: *(meine = MINE-uh)!*

Deutsch	Englisch
die Mutter - meine Mutter	mother - my mother
der Vater - mein Vater	father - my father
die Eltern - meine Eltern (pl.)	parents - my parents
der Sohn - sein Sohn	son - his son
die Tochter - seine Tochter	daughter - his daughter
der Bruder - ihr Bruder	brother - her brother
die Schwester - seine Schwester	sister - his sister
die Geschwister - meine Geschwister (pl.)	siblings / brothers and sisters - my brothers and sisters

die Großmutter - meine Großmutter	grandmother - my grandmother
die Oma - meine Oma	grandma/granny- my grandma
der Großvater - dein Großvater	grandfather - your grandfather
der Opa - sein Opa	grandpa - his grandpa
der Enkelsohn - mein Enkelsohn	grandson - my grandson
die Enkelin - seine Enkelin	granddaughter - his granddaughter

The Family

How you ask about someone's name or inquire about the family? Below are some common questions and answers in German and English.

Die Familie • The Family

Fragen and Antworten - Questions and Answers
Wie ist Ihr Name? - What's your name?

Deutsch	**English**
Wie heißen Sie?	What's your name? (formal)
Ich heiße Braun.	My name is Braun. (formal, last name)
Wie heißt du?	What's your name? (familiar)
Ich heiße Karla.	My name is Karla. (familiar, first name)
Wie heißt er/sie?	What's his/her name?

Er heißt Jones. His name is Jones. *(formal)*

Geschwister? - Siblings?

Haben Sie Geschwister? Do you have any brothers or sisters?

Ja, ich habe einen Bruder und eine Schwester. Yes, I have a / one brother and a / one sister.

Notice that you add -en to ein when you say you have a brother, and an -e for a sister. For now, just learn this as vocabulary.

Nein, ich habe keine Geschwister. No, I don't have any brothers or sisters.

Ja, ich habe zwei Schwestern. Yes, I have two sisters.

Wie heißt dein Bruder? What's your brother's name?

Er heißt Jens. His name is Jens. *(informal)*

Wie alt? - How old?

Wie alt ist dein Bruder? How old is your brother?

Er ist zehn Jahre alt. He is ten years old.

Wie alt bist du? How old are you? *(fam.)*

Ich bin zwanzig Jahre alt. I'm twenty years old.

YOU: du - Sie

As you study the vocabulary for this chapter, pay attention to the difference between asking a FORMAL ***(Sie)*** and a FAMILIAR ***(du/ihr)*** question. German-speakers tend to be much more formal than English-speakers. While Americans in particular may use first names with people they have just met or only know casually, German-speakers do not.

When a German-speaker is asked his or her name, the reply will be the last or family name, not the first name. The more formal question, **Wie ist Ihre Name?** as well as the standard **Wie heißen Sie?**, should be understood as 'what is your LAST name?'

Naturally, within the family and among good friends, the familiar 'you' pronouns **du** and **ihr** are used, and people are on a first-name basis. But when in doubt, you should always err on the side of being too formal, rather than too familiar.

Kultur

KLEINE FAMILIEN

Families in the German-speaking countries tend to be small, with only one or two children *(or no children)*. The birthrate in Austria, Germany and Switzerland is lower than in many modern industrialised nations, with fewer births than deaths, i.e., less than zero population growth.

Exercise

1. Complete the sentences logically in German as in the example.

BEISPIEL: Der Bruder von meinem Vater ist mein **Onkel**.

EXAMPLE: The brother of my father is my **uncle**.

1. Die Tochter von meiner Mutter ist meine __________.
2. Der Ehemann von meiner Tante ist mein __________.
3. Der Bruder von meiner Frau ist mein ___________.
4. Die Mutter von meinem Vater ist meine __________.
5. Die Tochter von meinem Sohn ist meine __________.
6. Der Sohn von meinem Vater ist mein ____________.
7. Der Vater von meiner Großmutter ist mein _________.

Answers

1. Die Tochter von meiner Mutter ist meine **Schwester**.
2. Der Ehemann von meiner Tante ist mein **Onkel**.
3. Der Bruder von meiner Frau ist mein **Schwager**.
4. Die Mutter von meinem Vater ist meine **Großmutter**.
5. Die Tochter von meinem Sohn ist meine **Enkelin**.
6. Der Sohn von meinem Vater ist mein **Bruder**.
7. Der Vater von meiner Großmutter ist mein **Urgroßvater**.

2. Answer the following questions in German:

1. Wie heißen Ihre Eltern? - ____________________
2. Haben Sie Geschwister? - ____________________
3. Wie alt ist Ihr Bruder/Ihre Schwester? - ________
4. Wie heißt deine Schwester/dein Bruder? - ______
5. Wie alt ist Ihr Vater? - ______________________
6. Wie heißt er? - ____________________________
7. Haben Sie eine Tante oder einen Onkel? Wie heißt sie/er? - ________________________________
8. Wie ist Ihre Name? - _________________________
9. Wie alt sind Sie? - __________________________

10. Wie heiβt du? - ______________________________

Answers

1. Wie heiβen Ihre Eltern?

Mein Vater heiβt Kevin. Meine Mutter heiβt Julie.

2. Haben Sie Geschwister?

Ja, ich habe eine Schwester. - **Ja, ich habe einen Bruder**.

Ja, ich habe zwei Schwestern und drei Brüder. (**eine groβe Familie**! = a large family!)

Nein, ich habe keine Geschwister. (**Ich bin Einzelkind**. = I'm an only child.)

3. Wie alt ist Ihr Bruder/Ihre Schwester? - **Er/Sie ist 12 Jahre alt**.

4 Wie heiβt deine Schwester/dein Bruder? - **Er/Sie heiβt Eric/Jane**.

5. Wie alt ist Ihr Vater? - **Mein Vater (Er) ist 45 Jahre alt**.

6. Wie heiβt er? - **Er heiβt Bob**.

7. Haben Sie eine Tante oder einen Onkel? Wie heiβt sie/er?

Ja, ich habe einen Onkel (eine Tante). Er (Sie) heiβt Onkel Hans (Tante Luise).

8. Wie ist Ihre Name? - **Ich heiβe Brown/Smith/McNeil**. (*formal, last name*)

8. *Alternate answer* Wie ist Ihr Name? - **Mein Name ist Brown/Smith/McNeil**.

9. Wie alt sind Sie? - **Ich bin 56 Jahre alt**. *(can you write out/say your age in German?)*

10. Wie heiβt du? - **Ich heiβe Judy/Sam/Maria**. *(familiar, first name)*

Lesson 13

Directions: How do I get there?

In this chapter, you'll learn vocabulary and grammar related to going places, asking for simple directions and receiving directions. You'll learn words and phrases that will let you talk about going places, as well as understand what someone else says when giving simple directions.

One word of caution before we begin. **Asking** for directions is easy. **Understanding** the torrent of German you may get back is another story! Most German textbooks/courses teach you how to **ask** the questions, but fail to deal adequately with the **understanding** aspect. That's why we will also teach you scme coping skills in this chapter to help in such situations. One example is to ask your question in such a way that it will elicit a simple **ja** or **nein**, or a simple 'left', 'straight ahead' or 'right' answer. And don't forget those ever-reliable hand signals that work in any language!

WO vs. WOHIN

German has two question words for asking 'where'. One *(**wo?**)* is for asking the **location** of someone or something. The other *(**wohin?**)* is for asking about **motion** or **direction** ('where to').

For instance, in English you would use 'where' to ask both 'Where are the keys?' (location) and 'Where are you going?' (motion/direction). In German these two questions require two different forms of 'where':

Wo sind die Schlüssel? *('Where are the keys?')*

Wohin gehen Sie? *('Where are you going?')*

In English this can be compared to the difference between the location question 'where's it at?' *(poor English, but it gets the idea across)* and the direction question 'where to?' But in German you can only use **wo?** for 'where's it at?' *(location)* and **wohin?** for 'where to?' *(direction)*. Sometimes **wohin** gets split in two, as in: '**Wo gehen Sie hin?**' But you can't use **wo** without **hin** to ask about motion or direction in German. - You must always use the correct form of 'where' for location *(**wo?**)* or motion/direction *(**wohin?**)*.

Now let's look at some common words and expressions related to directions and places we might go to. You need to memorize this vocabulary.

DIRECTIONS - RICHTUNGEN

Notice that in some of the phrases below, the gender *(der/die/das)* may affect the article, as in 'in die Kirche' or 'an den See'. Notice that *(der)* sometimes changes to *(den)*, and so on. For now, just notice what's going on related to gender!

English	**Deutsch**
along/down	entlang
Go along/down this street.	Gehen Sie diese Straße entlang!
back	zurück
Go back.	Gehen Sie zurück!
in the direction of/towards...	in Richtung auf...
the train station	den Bahnhof
the church	die Kirche
the hotel	das Hotel
left - to the left	links - nach links
right - to the right	rechts - nach rechts
straight ahead	geradeaus *(geh-RAH-duh-ows)*
Keep going straight ahead.	Gehen Sie immer geradeaus!
up to, until	bis zum *(masc./neut.)* bis zur *(fem.)*
up to the traffic light	bis zur Ampel
up to the cinema	bis zum Kino

Compass Directions

north - to the north	der Nord*(en)* - nach Norden
north of *(Leipzig)*	nördlich von *(Leipzig)*
south - to the south	der Süd*(en)* - nach Süden
south of *(Munich)*	südlich von *(München)*

east - to the east	der Ost*(en)* - nach Osten
east of (Frankfurt)	östlich von (Frankfurt)
west - to the west	der West(en) - nach Westen
west of (Cologne)	westlich von (Köln)

Note : More compass directions can be formed in German just as in English by combining more than one element. Northwest - Nordwesten, Northeast - Nordosten, Southwest - Südwesten, etc.

Lesson 14

Places to Go

In English we can say we're going **to** the bank, **to** Boston, or **to** Switzerland, but in German there is more than one way to say 'to'—and each one of these 'to' phrases would use a different German preposition. However, there are some rules and guidelines you can learn for these situations.

Most geographic place names *(countries, states, cities, etc.)* use **nach** for 'to'. Only a few countries that are feminine, masculine or plural *(rather than the normal neuter **das**)* use **in** for 'to'. Notice the exceptions listed below.

When going to a location in town, such as to the bakery or a restaurant, the most common prepositions for 'to' are **in** and **zu** *(usually in a compound such as **zum** or **zur**).*

English	**Deutsch**
IN DER STADT - IN TOWN	
to the supermarket	zum Supermarkt
from *(the bank)* to *(the hotel)*	von *(der Bank)* bis

from *(the hotel)* to *(the bank)*	*(zum Hotel)* von *(dem Hotel)* bis *(zur Bank)*
bakery - to the bakery	die Bäckerei - zur Bäckerei
bank - to the bank	die Bank - zur Bank
bar/pub - to the bar/pub	die Kneipe - in die Kneipe
butcher	der Fleischer/der Metzger
to the butcher	zum Fleischer/zum Metzger
hotel - to the hotel	das Hotel - zum Hotel
market/fleamarket	der Markt/der Flohmarkt
to the market	zum Markt/zum Flohmarkt
cinema - to the movies/cinema	das Kino - ins/zum Kino
the post office - to the post office	die Post - zur Post
restaurant - to the restaurant	das Restaurant - ins/zum Restaurant
to a/the Chinese restaurant	zum Chinesen
to an/the Italian restaurant	zum Italiener
to a/the Greek restaurant	zum Griechen
school - to school Schule	die Schule - zur
the shopping centre	das Einkaufszentrum
to the shopping centre	zum Einkaufszentrum
the traffic light/signal	die Ampel

(up) to the signal	bis zur Ampel
the train station - to the station	der Bahnhof - zum Bahnhof
work - to work	die Arbeit - zur Arbeit
the youth hostel to the youth hostel	die Jugendherberge in die Jugendherberge

ANDERSWO - ELSEWHERE

the lake - to the lake	der See - an den See
the sea - to the sea	die See/das Meer - ans Meer
the toilet/restroom	die Toilette/das Klo/das WC
to the toilet/restroom	auf die Toilette/zum Klo/zum WC

Note the following contractions in some of the phrases above : ins = in + das, 24m = 24 + den, 24r = 24 + der, ans = an + das

LÄNDER/STÄDTE - COUNTRIES/CITIES

from *(Frankfurt)* to *(Berlin)*	von *(Frankfurt)* nach *(Berlin)*
to... *(countries/cities)*	nach... *(Nationen/Städte)*
Germany	Deutschland
France	Frankreich
Australia	Australien
Munich	München
Berlin	Berlin
to Switzerland	in die Schweiz

to the US	in die USA
to Iran	in den Iran

Now here are some adverbs that tell us **when** we're going some place—along with sample sentences.

WANN? - WHEN?

GRAMMATIK: Notice that in German, TIME comes before PLACE! In English, it's the other way around. See the sample sentences below.

English	**Deutsch**
yesterday - today - tomorrow	gestern - heute - morgen
We're going to the cinema tomorrow.	Wir gehen morgen ins Kino.
(the) day before yesterday	vorgestern
(the) day after tomorrow	übermorgen
We're driving to Vienna *(the)* day after tomorrow.	Wir fahren übermorgen nach Wien.
this morning/afternoon	heute morgen/ nachmittag
He's travelling to Hamburg this morning.	Er fährt heute Morgen nach Hamburg.
now - later	jetzt - später
I'm going to work later.	Ich gehe später zur Arbeit.
at eight o'clock	um acht Uhr
I'm going to the station at eight.	Ich gehe um acht zum Bahnhof.

FRAGEN und ANTWORTEN
Questions and Answers in German and English

In the sentences below, the TO-phrases are in bold type – both in German and English. For now, learn the patterns for the various articles *(der/die/das)* for each gender *(masc./fem./neuter).*

Wohin fahren Sie? / Wohin fährst du?
Where are you going? *(driving/travelling)*

Ich fahre morgen an den See.
I'm going to the lake tomorrow.

Ich fahre morgen nach Dresden.
I'm going to Dresden tomorrow.

Wie komme ich...
How do I get...

...zur Bank? - Gehen Sie zwei Straßen und dann rechts.
...to the bank? - Go two blocks *(streets)* and then right.

...zum Hotel? - Fahren Sie diese Straße entlang.
...to the hotel? - Drive down/along this street.

...zur Post? - Gehen Sie bis zur Ampel und dann links.
...to the post office? - Go up to the traffic light and then left.

Note : For the items above, if you are **walking**, you use gehen; if you are **driving**, you use fahren.

Extra-Ausdrücke
Extra Expressions

an der Kirche vorbei past the church
am Kino vorbei past the cinema

rechts/links an der Ampel
right/left at the traffic light

am Marktplatz at the market square
an der Ecke at the corner

die nächste Straße the next street
über die Straße across/over the street

über den Marktplatz across the market square
vor dem Bahnhof
in front of the train station

vor der Kirche
in front of the church

Exercise

1.WOHIN? - Answer logically in German, using the English cue given. Make sure to respond correctly according to the person being asked. See the examples below:

BEISPIEL A: **Wo gehst du hin?** *(cinema)* - **Ich gehe ins Kino**.

BEISPIEL B: **Wohin fahren wir?** *(Bonn)* - **Wir fahren nach Bonn**.

1. Wohin gehen Sie jetzt? *(toilet)* ____________________.
2. Wo fahren Sie hin? *(post office)* ________________.
3. Wohin geht Alex jetzt? *(bakery)* ________________.
4. Und wo gehst du denn hin? *(pub)* ______________.
5. Wohin gehen wir heute? *(Italian restaurant)* __________.
6. Wo fahren Sie hin? *(train station)* _______________.
7. Wohin gehen Andrea und Brigitte jetzt? *(shopping center)* ____.
8. Wohin fahren Sie morgen? *(London)* ____________.
9. Wohin geht Herr Schmidt jetzt? *(work)* __________.
10. Wohin fährst du jetzt? *(the lake)* ________________.

Answers

1. Wohin gehen Sie jetzt? *(toilet)* - **Ich gehe jetzt zur Toilette**. (or: **zum/aufs Klo / zum WC**)

2. Wo fahren Sie hin? *(post office)* - **Ich fahre zur Post**.

3. Wohin geht Alex jetzt? *(bakery)* - **Er geht jetzt zur Bäckerei**.

4. Und wo gehst du denn hin? *(pub)* - **Ich gehe in die Kneipe.**

5. Wohin gehen wir heute? *(Italian restaurant)* - **Wir gehen heute zum Italiener.**

6. Wo fahren Sie hin? *(train station)* - **Ich fahre zum Bahnhof.**

7. Wohin gehen Andrea und Brigitte jetzt? *(shopping center)* - **Sie [they] gehen jetzt zum Einkaufszentrum.**

8. Wohin fahren Sie morgen? *(London)* - **Ich fahre morgen nach London.**

9. Wohin geht Herr Schmidt jetzt? *(work)* - **Er geht jetzt zur Arbeit.**

10. Wohin fährst du jetzt? *(the lake)* - **Ich fahre an den See.**

2. zur oder zum?

Decide if the sentence requires **zur** or **zum** and fill in the blank:

1. Wie komme ich _____ Kirche?
2. Karl geht jetzt _____ Bahnhof.
3. Gehen Sie hier links und dann bis _____ Ampel
4. Wann geht er _____ Arbeit?
5. Karl geht heute _____ Markt.

Answers

1. Wie komme ich **zur** Kirche?
2. Karl geht jetzt **zum** Bahnhof.
3. Gehen Sie hier links und dann bis **zur** Ampel
4. Wann geht er **zur** Arbeit?
5. Karl geht heute **zum** Markt.

3. GEOGRAPHIE - Using the key below, fill in the correct answer in German. The following items require a basic knowledge of European geography. Please consult an atlas or map if you need to.

KEY: **a.** nördlich **b.** südlich **c.** östlich **d.** westlich

1. Frankreich liegt ___ von Deutschland.
2. Hamburg liegt ___ von Frankfurt.
3. Berlin liegt ___ von Dresden.
4. Österreich liegt ___ von Deutschland.
5. Österreich liegt ___ von der Schweiz.

Answers

1. Frankreich liegt **westlich** von Deutschland. *(d, west of)*
2. Hamburg liegt **nördlich** von Frankfurt. *(a, north of)*
3. Bremen liegt **nördlich** von München. *(a, north of)*
4. Österreich liegt **südlich** von Deutschland. *(b, south of)*
5. Österreich liegt **östlich** von der Schweiz. *(c, east of)*

Lesson 15

Give and Take - The Accusative Case

Command Forms

geben *(to give)* / **esgibt** *(there is/are)* **nehmen** (to take)/ **er nimmt** *(he takes)*

In this chapter you'll learn how to express in German the concepts of giving ***(geben)*** and taking ***(nehmen)***. This involves the grammatical elements known as the **accusative case** *(the direct object case in German)*, irregular **stem-changing verbs** and the **command forms** *(imperative)*. If that sort of grammar terminology scares you, don't worry. We'll introduce it all in such a way that you'll hardly feel a thing.

The important thing is that after studying this chapter, you'll be able to express the important and useful concepts of giving and taking.

geben (to give) - nehmen (to take)

These two German verbs have something in common. See if you can find what it is by observing the following:

geben

ich gebe *(I give)*, **du gibst** *(you give)*
er gibt *(he gives)*, **sie gibt** *(she gives)*
wir geben *(we give)*, **sie geben** *(they give)*

nehmen
ich nehme *(I take)*, **du nimmst** *(you take)*
er nimmt *(he takes)*, **sie nimmt** *(she takes)*
wir nehmen *(we take)*, **sie nehmen** *(they take)*

Now can you tell what essential change these two verbs have in common?

If you said that they both change from **e** to **i** in the same situations, then you're right! *(The verb **nehmen** also changes its spelling slightly, but the **e**-to-**i** change is what these two verbs have in common.)* Both of these verbs belong to a class of German verbs known as 'stem-changing' verbs. In the infinitive form (ending in -**en**) they have an **e** in their stem, or base form. But when they are conjugated (used with a pronoun or noun in a sentence), the stem vowel changes under certain conditions from **e** to **i**: **nehmen** (infinitive) —> **er nimmt** (conjugated, 3rd person sing.); **geben** (infinitive) —> **er gibt** (conjugated, 3rd person sing.)

All stem-changing verbs only change their stem vowel in the singular. Most only change when used with **er**, **sie**, **es** (3rd person) and **du** (*2nd person, familiar*). Other **e**-to-**i** stem-changing verbs include: **helfen/hilft** (*help*), **treffen/trifft** (meet) and **sprechen/spricht** (*speak*).

Now study the chart below. It shows all the forms of the two verbs in the present tense—in English and German. In the example sentences, observe also how direct objects (the things you give or take) that are masculine (***der***) change to **den** or **einen** when they function as direct objects *(rather than the subject)*. In the **accusative** *(direct object)* case, **der** is the only gender that has this change. Neuter (**das**), feminine (**die**) and plural nouns are unaffected.

The STEM-CHANGING Verbs
geben - nehmen

The words me, us, them (mir, uns, ihnen) and so on in the sentences with geben are indirect objects in the dative case. You will learn more about the dative in a future chapter. For now, just learn these words as vocabulary.

English	**Deutsch**
to give	geben
there is/there are	es gibt
Today there are no apples.	Heute gibt es keine Äpfel.

The expression es gibt (there is/are) always takes the accusative case: 'Heute gibt es keinen Wind'. = 'There is no wind today'.

I give	ich gebe
I give her the new ball.	Ich gebe ihr den neuen Ball.
you *(fam.)* give	du gibst
Are you giving him the money?	Gibst du ihm das Geld?
he gives	er gibt
He gives me the green book.	Er gibt mir das grüne Buch.
she gives	sie gibt
She gives us a book.	Sie gibt uns ein
Buch.	we give wir geben
	We aren't giving

them any kein — Wir geben ihnen money. Geld.

you (pl.) give — ihr gebt
You (guys) give me a key. — Ihr gebt mir einen Schlüssel.

they give — sie geben
They give him no opportunity. — Sie geben ihm keine Gelegenheit.

you (formal) give — Sie geben
Are you giving me the pencil? — Geben Sie mir den Bleistift?

to take nehmen

I take — ich nehme
I take the ball. — Ich nehme den Ball.

you (*fam.)* take — du nimmst
Are you taking the money? — Nimmst du das Geld?

he takes — er nimmt
He's taking the green book. — Er nimmt das grün Buch.

she takes — sie nimmt
She takes a book. — Sie nimmt ein Buch.

we take — wir nehmen
We aren't taking any money. — Wir nehmen kein Geld.

you (pl.) take — ihr nehmt
You (guys) take a key. — Ihr nehmt einen Schlüssel.

they take — sie nehmen
They take everything. — Sie nehmen alles.

you (formal) take — Sie nehmen

Are you taking the pencil?	Nehmen Sie den Bleistift?

By their nature, these two verbs are often used in the imperative *(command)* form. Below you'll find how to say things like 'Give me the pen!' or 'Take the money!' If you are talking to one person, the command will be different than if you are addressing two or more people. Note that, as usual, German makes a distinction between a formal **Sie** *(sing. and pl.)* command and a familiar **du** *(sing.)* or **ihr** *(pl.)* command. If you tell a child to give you something, the command will not be the same as when you are addressing an adult formally (***Sie***). If you are telling more than one child (**ihr**) to do something, that will also be a different command than if you are only addressing one child (**du**). The **du** command form of most verbs is almost always the normal **du** form of the verb minus the **-st** ending. ***(Du nimmst das Buch.*** ***- Nimm das Buch!)*** Study the chart below.

IMPERATIVE
Command Forms for
geben - nehmen

The German imperative verb forms vary according to whom you are commanding or telling to do something. Each form of YOU in German *(du, ihr, Sie)* has its own command form. Note that only the Sie command includes the pronoun in the command! The du and ihr commands do not usually include du or ihr.

English	**Deutsch**
	geben
Give me the *(ballpoint)* pen! *(Sie)*	Geben Sie mir den Kuli!
Give me the (ballpoint) pen! (du)	Gib mir den Kuli!

Give me the (ballpoint) pen! (ihr)	Gebt mir den Kuli!
	(nehmen)
Take the (ballpoint) pen! (Sie)	Nehmen Sie den Kuli!
Take the (ballpoint) pen! (du)	Nimm den Kuli!
Take the (ballpoint) pen! (ihr)	Nehmt den Kuli!

Try the following exercises to see if you have learned how to conjugate and use the German verbs **geben** and **nehmen** in a sentence. Note that when you use these two verbs, you often have a direct object in the **accusative case**. Before you begin, study the following chart—a brief overview of the accusative case:

Nominative (Subject)	Accusative (Object)	Beispiele (Examples)
der	den	**Der Bleistift** ist hier. (nom.) Er gibt mir **den Bleistift**. (acc.)
ein (masc.)	einen	**Sein Wagen** ist blau. (nom., der Wagen)
kein	keinen	Nimmst du **seinen blauen Wagen**? (acc.)
er (he)	ihn (him)	**Er** ist hier. (nom.) Nimmst du **ihn**? (acc.)

Note : The masculine gender (der/er) is the only one that changes in the accusative case. Neither the plural nor the feminine (die) and neuter (das) genders change in the accusative. But der becomes den, er becomes ihn, and ein changes to einen *(kein/keinen, mein/meinen, etc.)*.

Exercise

A. geben

Write a complete sentence in German using the elements shown. Follow the examples. For items with a question mark, make the sentence a question. Add any necessary endings and make any needed changes to form a complete sentence.

Beispiel: wir / geben / ihm / ein Buch - **Wir geben ihm ein Buch**.

Beispiel: geben / du / ihm / der Kuli ? - **Gibst du ihm den Kuli**?

1. er / geben / mir / ein Radio
2. geben / wir / ihr / ein Auto ?
3. geben / du / mir / kein Bleistift ?
4. ihr / geben / uns / der Film
5. Maria / geben / ihm / ein Bier

Answers

1. er / geben / mir / ein Radio = Er gibt mir ein Radio. (He's giving me a radio.)
2. geben / wir / ihr / ein Auto ? = Geben wir ihr ein Auto? (Are we giving her a car?)
3. geben / du / mir / kein Bleistift ? = Gibst du mir keinen Bleistift? (Aren't you giving me a pencil?)
4. ihr / geben / uns / der Film = Ihr gebt uns den Film. (You guys are giving us the film.)
5. Maria / geben / ihm / ein Bier = Maria gibt ihm ein Bier. (Maria's giving him a beer.)

B. nehmen

Write a complete sentence in German using the elements shown. Use the following example as a model.

For items with a question mark, make the sentence a question. Add any necessary endings and make any needed changes to form a complete sentence.

Beispiel: Sie / nehmen / der Wein - **Sie nehmen den Wein**.

6. nehmen / du / der Ball ?
7. ich / nehmen / kein Schlüssel [key]
8. er / nehmen / der Bleistift
9. Sie / nehmen / ein Kuli
10. nehmen / Karl und Heike / ein Buch ?

Answers

6. nehmen / du / der Ball ? = Nimmst du den Ball?
7. ich / nehmen / kein Schlüssel = Ich nehme keinen Schlüssel.
8. er / nehmen / der Belistift = Er nimmt den Bleistift.
9. Sie / nehmen / ein Kuli = Sie nehmen einen Kuli.
10. nehmen / Karl und Heike / ein Buch ? = Nehmen Karl und Heike ein Buch?

C. es gibt

Translate the English into a German sentence using **es gibt** and the word indicated. Follow the example. Some items will use **kein** *(not any, none)*.

Beispiel: Is there a calendar? *(der Kalender)* - **Gibt es einen Kalender**?

11. Is there no money? *(das Geld)*
12. There's a difference. *(der Unterschied)*
13. There's no wind. *(der Wind)*
14. Is there time? *(die Zeit)*
15. There's no time. *(die Zeit)*

Answers

11. Is there no money? *(das Geld)* = Gibt es kein Geld?
12. There's a difference. *(der Unterschied)* = Es gibt einen Unterschied.
13. There's no wind. *(der Wind)* = Es gibt keinen Wind.
14. Is there time? *(die Zeit)* = Gibt es Zeit?
15. There's no time. *(die Zeit)* = Es gibt keine Zeit.

D. Befehlsform *(command form)*

Write a command in German using the verb and form indicated ***(du, ihr, Sie** commands)*. Follow the examples.

Beispiel: geben *(du)* / ihm / der Kuli - **Gib ihm den Kuli**!

Beispiel: nehmen *(Sie)* / der Kuli - **Nehmen Sie den Kuli**!

16. nehmen *(ihr)* / der Bleistift
17. geben *(Sie)* / mir / das Buch
18. nehmen *(du)* / der Wagen
19. geben *(du)* / ihm / der Wein
20. nehmen *(Sie)* / die Tasche [bag]

Answers

16. nehmen *(ihr)* / der Bleistift = Nehmt den Bleistift! (Take the pencil!)
17. geben *(Sie)* / mir / das Buch = Geben Sie mir das Buch! *(Give me the book!)*
18. nehmen *(du)* / der Wagen = Nimm den Wagen! *(Take the car!)*
19. geben ***(du)*** / ihm / der Wein = Gib ihm den Wein! *(Give him the wine!)*
20. nehmen *(Sie)* / die Tasche = Nehmen Sie die Tasche! *(Take the bag!)*

Lesson 16

German Menu And Dining Guide

A German-English Glossary for Food and Drink

The following menu and dining guide contains an alphabetical glossary of words and expressions that are likely to be encountered on a typical menu (**die Speisekarte**) in Austria, Germany or Switzerland. Keep in mind that, as with many things in the German-speaking world, food and drink vocabulary is regional. Some dishes are more likely to be found in one part of Germany and not in another. Certain regions tend to have more beer or tea drinkers, while others may prefer coffee or wine. If you look at a menu in Munich, it will be very different from one in Hamburg. However, there are many things they will have in common and we offer a wide range of selections on our *Speisekarte*. We have also included some related terms and the words for places to eat and drink. **Guten Appetit!**

Food Preparation

English	Deutsch
baked	*(im Ofen)* gebacken
boiled	gekocht
cold	kalt
(deep) fried	*(fritiert)* gebacken
(pan) fried	*(in der Pfanne)* gebacken
hot	heiß
hot *(spicy)*	scharf
medium *(done)*	halbdurch
rare	englisch
well done	durchgebraten
roasted	gebraten
seasoned	gewürzt
smoked	geräuchert
steamed	gedämpft
stuffed	gefüllt

A

Aal eel

Abend essen

Abendessen dinner, supper

alkoholfrei *(adj.)* non-alcoholic

Ananas pineapple

Apfel apple

Ein Glas Apfelsaft a glass of apple juice

Apfelkuchen apple cake

Apfelmost (hard) apple cider

Apfelmus apple sauce

Apfelsaft apple juice

Apfelsaftschorle apple spritzer *(apple juice or cider mixed with sparkling mineral water; the standard* ***Schorle*** *found in southwest Germany is made with wine)*

Apfelsine orange

Apfelstrudel apple strudel

Apfeltasche apple turnover, apple pie

Apfelwein cider

Called *Ebbelwei* or *Eppelwoi* in the local dialect, this fermented cider drink is a specialty of the Frankfurt am Main area.

Aprikose*(n)* apricot*(s)*

Aubergine eggplant

Auflauf soufflé

Austern oysters

B

Backhendel roasted chicken *(Austria)*

Barbe mullet *(fish)*

Basilikum basil *(seasoning)*

Beilage*(n)* side dish*(es)*

Beisl/Beisel inn, pub, small restaurant *(Austria)*

belegtes Brot open-faced sandwich

Besteck (das) cutlery
die Gabel fork
der Löffel spoon
das Messer knife

bestellen to order

Bestellung order
auf Bestellung made to order, on request

Bier beer

One rarely orders just a 'beer' in Germany. Try to be specific, and order by brand or type *(pils, bock, dunkel, hell, weizen, etc.)*. Germans tend to drink beer from a local brewery.

Birne*(n)* pear*(s)*

blau (adj.) boiled *(in salt and vinegar)*, usually fish
Blaubeeren blueberries

Blumenkohl cauliflower

Bockbier bock beer

Bock beer - usually a dark, strong, sweeter brew - gets its name from 'Bock', derived from the town of Einbeck in Lower Saxony (Niedersachsen), known for its hops beer. Bock is traditionally brewed in the fall and aged through the winter for consumption in the spring. A stronger variety is called Doppelbock.

Bockwurst bockwurst *(sausage)*

Bohnen beans

Bowle punch
Apfelwein-Bowle cider punch
Berliner Bowle a punch made of Berliner Weiße beer and champagne

Brat- fried, roasted
Brathähnchen fried chicken
Bratkartoffeln fried potatoes
Bratwurst fried sausage

Brombeeren blackberries

Brot bread

There are over 200 kinds of German bread

Brötchen rolls

In southern Germany 'rolls' are called *Semmeln*.

Buletten meatballs

Butter butter

C

Champagner champagne

Champignons *(button)* mushrooms

Pilze mushrooms

Pfifferlinge chanterelle mushrooms

Schwammerl mushrooms (*Austria*)

D

deutsches Beefsteak hamburger

Doboschtorte a seven-layer cake with mocha cream

Dorsch/Kabeljau cod

dunkel dark *(beer)*

Dunkelbier dark beer

ein Dunkles a dark beer

ein Helles a light beer

E

Ei (Eier) egg *(eggs)*

mit Schinken with ham

mit Speck with bacon

ein hartgekochtes Ei a hard-boiled egg

ein weichgekochtes Ei a soft-boiled egg

Rührei scrambled eggs

Spiegeleier fried eggs

eingelegt *(adj.)* pickled

Eintopf stew

Eis ice; ice cream
ein Erdbeereis a serving of strawberry ice cream
ein Vanilleeis a serving of vanilla ice cream
Himbeereis raspberry ice cream
Schokoladeneis chocolate ice cream

Ente duck

Erbsen peas
Erbsensuppe pea soup

Erdapfel ***(Erdäpfel)*** potato(es) (*Austria*)

Erdbeeren strawberries

Erdnub peanut
Erdnubbutter peanut butter

Essig vinegar
Öl und Essig oil and vinegar

Estragon tarragon *(seasoning)*

F

Fasan pheasant

Faschiertes ground meat *(Austria)*

Fett fat; grease

Flammekuchen 'flame cake', thin layer of pastry topped with cream, onions and bacon. Sometimes cheese and/ or mushrooms are added to this baked dish.

Fleisch meat
Kalbfleisch veal
Rindfleisch beef

Schweinefleisch pork

Fleischerei butcher shop

Flunder flounder

Forelle trout
Frikadelle meat balls, rissole

frittiert *(adj.)* fried
frittierte Zwiebelringe fried onion rings

Froschschenkel frogs legs

Frucht fruit
Fruchtsaft fruit juice

Frühstück breakfast

G

Gabel fork

Gans goose

Goose is a traditional Christmas or special occasion dish, although it is being overtaken by turkey - *Pute*.

Gaststätte restaurant

Garnelen shrimp
Garnelencocktail shrimp cocktail

Gemüse*(n)* vegetable*(s)*

Geröstete (Erdäpfel) roasted, fried potatoes (*Austria*)
Same as 'Bratkartoffeln'

Geschnetzeltes meat cut into strips stewed to produce a thick sauce.

Geselchtes, Gselchtes smoked meat, usually pork (*Austria*)

Gespritzte*(r)* spritzer, wine cooler (*Austria/Bavaria*)
Schorle mix, wine and soda water

Gewürz*(e)* seasoning*(s)*, spice*(s)*

Grapefruit grapefruit
Grapefruitsaft grapefruit juice

grillen (v.) to grill, barbecue
gegrillt grilled, barbecued
Grillteller grill plate

Grütze groats
rote Grütze red fruit pudding
Grieß semolina
Grießklößchen semolina dumpling
Grießkoch, - brei semolina purée

Gulasch goulash *(veal stew with spices)*

Gurke*(n)* cucumber*(s)*
saure Gurken pickled, gherkins

H

Hackbraten meatloaf
Hackepeter hamburger steak
Hackfleisch ground meat, minced meat

Hähnchen, **Huhn** chicken
Hendl Austrian for chicken
ein halbes Hähnchen a half chicken

Hühnerbrust chicken breast
Hühnerbruststreifen chicken breast strips

Hühnersuppe chicken soup

halbtrocken semi-dry *(wine)*

Hase rabbit
Hasenpfeffer jugged hare

Hauptspeisen entrées, main courses

hausgemacht *(adj.)* home made

Haxe leg of *(lamb, pork, etc.)*
Lammshaxe leg of lamb
Schweinshaxe pork's knuckle

Heilbutt halibut
heiß *(adj.)* hot
heiße Schokolade hot chocolate

Hendl chicken *(Austria)*
Backhendl roasted chicken

Himbeeren raspberries
Himbeereis raspberry ice cream
Himbeersaft raspberry juice

Honig honey

Hummer lobster

J

Jägerschnitzel cutlet served with mushroom sauce

Jause snack (*Austria*), afternoon tea

Joghurt yogurt

Johannisbeeren currants (red, black)

Johannisbrot carob *(bean)*, St. John's bread

K

Kabeljau cod
Kaffee coffee
Kaffee mit Sahne coffee with cream
Kaffee mit Zucker coffee with sugar
koffeinfreier Kaffee decaf

Kalb- veal *(in compound words)*
Kalbfleisch veal

Kaninchen rabbit

Karotten carrots

Kartoffel*(n)* potato(es)
Bratkartoffeln fritters, roasted potatoes
Kartoffelbrei, -püree mashed potatoes
Pommes frites French fried potatoes
Salzkartoffeln (salt) boiled potatoes

Käse ***(der)*** cheese

Käsesorten
Types of Cheese

Deutsch	**English**
Blauschimmelkäse	Blue cheese
Chesterkäse	Cheshire
Emmenthaler	Swiss cheese
Hüttenkäse	cottage cheese
Schimmelkäse	Gorgonzolla
Ziegenkäse	goat's milk cheese

Kasseler Rippchen smoked pork rib

Kellner waiter
Kellnerin waitress
Herr Ober! Waiter!

Fräulein! **used to be an acceptable way to get the attention of your waitress. Today it is considered sexist, and Germans avoid using it. Unfortunately, there is no good replacement, so people generally resort to hand-waving instead. 'Herr Ober!' isn't sexist, but it only works for males and is a bit old-fashioned.**

Ketchup ketchup

Kiwi kiwi

Klopse meat balls (*N. Germany*)

Kneipe bar, pub

Knoblauch garlic

Knödel dumpling*(s)*

Kokosnub coconut

Kompott stewed fruit

Konditorei pastry shop, cake shop

Korn grain

Vollkornbrot whole meal bread, whole wheat bread

Kotelett cutlet, chop

Konfitüre jam

Krabben shrimps

Krapfen doughnut*(s)*, fritter*(s)*

Krebs crawfish, crab

Kren horseradish (*Austria*)

Kuchen cake

Kümmel caraway

L

Lachs salmon

Laibchen meat balls or dumplings (*Austria*)

Lamm lamb

Languste *(rawfish)*

Leber liver

Leberkäse lit., 'liver-cheese', but this type of large sausage *(usually served hot)* is difficult to translate. Sometimes translated as 'meatloaf', it is more like a loaf of smooth sausage. Bought at the local butcher, it has a soft, firm consistency and a salty, cold-cut taste.

Leberknödel liver dumplings

Leberwurst liversausage

Lendensteak sirloin steak

lieblich sweet *(wine)*

Limonade (Limo) lemonade

Linsen lentils

Linsensuppe lentil soup

Löffel spoon

Lorbeerblatt bayleaf *(seasoning)*

M

Mais corn, maize

Mandeln almonds

Marille*(n)* apricot*(s)* (*Austria*)

Marmelade jam, marmalade

The German word *Marmelade*, is less specific than English 'marmalade' - which is usually only a citrus jam with rinds. The German word may refer to any jam, jelly or preserves, although there are more specific words, such as *Konfitüre*.

Maronen chestnuts

Maß a liter *of beer*

Matjes herring

Maultaschen ravioli *(Swabian version)*

Meeresfrüchte seafood

Meerrettich horseradish

Mehlspeise cake; dessert (*Austria*)

Melanzani eggplant (*Austria*)

Melone melon

Menü special of the day, set menu

Do not confuse this word with *Speisekarte*, the printed menu. *Das Menü* is a set combination of items from the menu at a special price. There may be several offered each day.

Messer knife (*also see* ***Besteck***)

Metzgerei butcher shop

Milch milk

Milchcafé milk coffee,

Mineralwasser mineral water,
mit/ohne Kohlensäure carbonated/non-carbonated
stilles Wasser non-carbonated water

Mittagessen lunch, midday meal

Mohrrüben carrots

Most hard cider, fruit wine

Muscheln mussels
Muskatnuß nutmeg

N

Nachspeise dessert
Nachtisch dessert

Nieren kidneys

Nockerl dumplings (*Austria/Bavaria*)
Salzburger Nockerl a sweet, light, dumpling soufflé

Nudeln noodles

Nutella Nutella - A dark, creamy chocolate-almond paste popular in Germany for making sandwiches or spreading on crackers. Sold in tubes and jars like peanut butter.

O

Ober waiter,

Herr Ober! Waiter!

Obst fruit

Obstsalat fruit salad

Ochsenschwanzsuppe oxtail soup

Öl oil

P

Pampelmuse grapefruit
Often called 'Grapefruit' in German

paniert (adj.) breaded (*Wienerschnitzel*, etc.)

Paprika paprika *(in Switz.)*

Parmaschinken prosciutto *(ham)*
Parmaschinken mit Melone prosciutto with melon

Peperoni chillies

Do not order a *Peperoni-Pizza* in Germany unless you really want a pizza with a hot chili pepper topping! If you want something closer to the US pepperoni pizza, order a *Salami-Pizza*.

Petersilie parsley

Pfand deposit for bottles or glasses (*in a beer garden or at a stand)*

Pfannkuchen pancakes
Berliner Pfannkuchen type of doughnut

Pfeffer pepper

Pfirsiche peaches

Pflaumen plums

Pils pilsner *(beer)*

Pilze mushrooms
Champignons (button) mushrooms
Pfifferlinge chanterelle mushrooms
Schwammerl*(n)* mushroom*(s)* (*Austria*)
Steinpilze types of mushrooms

Pizza pizza *(Ger. pron. PITS-uh)*

Plätzchen cookies, biscuits (*Brit.*)

Pommes frites french fries, chips

Portion(en) portion*(s)*, serving*(s)*

Preis*(e)* price*(s)*

Preiselbeeren cranberries

Pute turkey (hen)
Puter *(cock)* turkey
Putenschnitzel breaded turkey breast (*Wienerschnitzel* made with turkey rather than veal or pork)

R

Radieschen radish*(es)*

Radler/Radlermass beer and lemonade or soda pop

Rechnung bill, check

Reh/Hirsch venison

Reis rice

Rhabarber rhubarb

Rind- beef *(in compounds)*
Rindfleisch beef

roh (*adj.)* raw

Romagna-Salat caesar salad

Rosinen raisins

Rotbarsch rose fish

rote Grütze red fruit pudding

Rührei scrambled eggs

Rum rum

S

Sachertorte Austrian cake with chocolate and whipped cream

Named for the Hotel Sacher in Vienna

Saft juice

saftig *(adj.)* juicy

Sahne cream,

Jahrezeit season

je nach jahrezeit depending on the season

Salami salami

Salamipizza pepperoni pizza

Salat salad, lettuce

Gurkensalat cucumber salad

Kartoffelsalat potato salad

Salz salt

Salzkartoffeln *(salt)* boiled potatoes

Sandwich sandwich

Sardellen anchovies

Sauce, **Soße** gravy, sauce

Sauer- pickled, sour

Sauerbraten sauerbraten, marinated beef

saure Gurken pickled gherkins

Sauerkraut sauerkraut, pickled cabbage

Sauerrahm sour cream

sauer, säuerlich *(adj.)* sour

scharf *(adj.)* hot, spicy

Schinken ham

Schlachtplatte cold cuts and sausage platter

Schlagsahne whipped cream
mit Schlag with whipped cream, topping

Schnaps liquor, schnapps

Schnecken snails, escargots

Schnellimbib shack - bar

Schnittkäse sliced cheese
Schnittlauch chives

Schnitzel cutlet, schnitzel
Jägerschnitzel cutlet served with mushroom sauce
Wiener Schnitzel breaded veal/pork cutlet
Zigeunerschnitzel cutlet with spicy sauce of red and green peppers

Schokolade chocolate
heiße Schokolade hot chocolate

Schorle wine and soda water mix
Gespritzte*(r)* spritzer, wine cooler *(Austria, Bavaria)*

Schwarzwälder Kirschtorte Black Forest cherry cake *(with cherry schnapps)*

Schweins- pork (in compound words)
Schweinskotelett pork chops
vom Schwein from the pig,

Schweinefleisch pork

Seezunge sole

Sekt sparkling wine

Semmel*(n)* bread roll*(s)* *(Austria, So. Ger.)*
Semmelknödel bread dumplings *(Austria, So. Ger.)*

Senf mustard

Serviette napkin, serviette

Sesam sesame *(seasoning)*

Spargel asparagus

German asparagus is usually white rather than green. It is cultivated with a covering of earth to keep it pale, and is considered a delicacy in several regions in June.

Spätzle type of S. German/Bavarian pasta *(often instead of potatoes)*

Speck bacon

Speisekarte menu

Spezialität des Hauses specialty of the house

Spiegeleier fried eggs

Spieß spit, skewer
vom Spieß shish kebab

Spinat spinach

Stachelbeeren gooseberries

Steak steak
Steak Tatar, **Tatarbeefsteak** steak tartare, raw steak

Straubwirtschaft seasonal wine room
Besenwirtschaft another word for *Straubwirtschaft*

Sülze diced meat or fish in aspic; brawn

Suppe soup

süss sweet

T

Tafelspitz cooked beef with horseradish and cream sauce

Tagesgericht dish of the day, today's entrée

Tagessuppe soup of the day

Tasse cup

Tatar tartare

Taube pigeon, dove

Tee tea

Tee mit Milch tea with cream/milk

Tee mit Zitrone tea with lemon

Teller plate

Thunfisch tuna fish

Tintenfisch squid

Tomate tomato

Tomatensaft tomato juice

Tomatensuppe tomato soup

Torte cake, tart

Trauben grapes

Traubensaft grape juice

Trinkgeld tip

trocken *(adj.)* dry (*wine)*

Truthahn turkey

V

vegetarisch *(adj.)* vegetarian

verlorene Eier poached eggs

Vollkornbrot whole wheat/meal bread

Vorspeise*(n)* starter*(s)*, hors d'oeuvre*(s)*

W

Waldfrüchte wild *(forest)* berries

Wachtel quail

Wasser water
Leitungswasser tap water
Mineralwasser mineral water,
stilles Wasser non-carbonated water

Wassermelone watermelon

Wein wine
Rotwein red wine
Weißwein white wine

Weintrauben grapes

Wurst, sausage, small sausage Würstchen

Weinstube wine room, wine bar

Weißbrot white bread

Weißkohl cabbage

Weizenbier wheat beer

Wermut vermouth

Mettwurst soft smoked sausage, usually pork

Wurst, the German national food, comes in an amazing number of varieties. The four main types *(based on how they are made)* are: *(1)* Rohwurst *(Salami, Mettwurst)*, *(2)* Brühwurst *(Fleischwurst, Frankfurter)*, *(3)* Kochwurst *(Leberwurst, Prebkopf)* and *(4)* Bratwurst *(for cooking)*.

Z

Zahnstocher toothpick
Zimt cinnamon

Zitrone lemon

Zucker sugar

Zwetsche*(n)*, Zwetschge*(n)* plum*(s)*
Zwetschgenknödel plum dumpling
Zwetschenschnaps, -wasser plum brandy

Zwiebel*(n)* onion*(s)*
fritierte Zwiebelringe fried onion rings

Zwiebelsuppe onion soup

Some useful words and expressions in English and German

Places to Eat or Drink

Deutsch	**English**
die Bar	bar, pub
das Gasthaus	inn, small restaurant
die Gaststätte	inn, small restaurant
die Kneipe	bar, pub
das Lokal	bar, pub; restaurant
das Restaurant	restaurant
	inn, small restaurant
beim Chinesen	at the Chinese restaurant
beim Griechen	at the Greek restaurant
beim Italiener	at the Italian restaurant

Useful Phrases

English	**Deutsch**
I'd like...	**Ich möchte...**
A menu, please!	**Eine Speisekarte, bitte!**

What do you recommend?	**Was empfehlen Sie?**
What would you like to drink?	**Was möchten Sie trinken?**
with / without	**mit / ohne**
Is this table/seat free?	**Ist dieser Tisch/Platz noch frei?**
I didn't order that.	**Das habe ich nicht bestellt.**
Cheers!	**Prost!**
Your health !	**Auf Ihr Wohl!**
Check, please.	**Zahlen, bitte.** **Die Rechnung, bitte.**
All together, please.	**Bitte alles zusammen.**
Separate bills, please.	**Getrennt, bitte.** **Getrennte Rechnungen, bitte.**

Lesson 17

The Table Setting: Plates, cups, cutlery, etc.

What do we find on a table set for dining? Below is an English-German chart of various items that might be found on a typical dining table.

Der gedeckte Tisch
Useful words and expressions
in English and German

ENGLISH	**DEUTSCH**
CUTLERY	**DAS BESTECK**
fork	die Gabel
knife	das Messer
spoon	der Löffel
teaspoon	der Teelöffel
tablespoon	der Eblöffel
cake	der Tortenheber

CHINA, DISHES	**DAS GESCHIRR**
bowl	die Schale,
cup/mug	die Tasse/der Becher
saucer	die Untertasse
plate, salad plate	der Teller, der Salatteller

CONTAINERS	**BEHÄLTER**
can - beer can, coke can	die Dose - Bierdose, Coladose
a can of beer/coke	eine Dose Bier/Cola
glass - beer glass, wine glass	das Glas - Bierglas, Weinglas
a glass of beer/wine/milk	ein Glas Bier/Wein/ Milch
bottle - beer bottle, wine bottle	die Flasche - Bierflasche, Weinflasche
a bottle of beer/wine/milk	eine Flasche Bier/ Wein/ Milch
a cup of coffee/tea	eine Tasse Kaffee/Tee
a cup of ice cream	ein*(en)* Becher Eis
dish, *(serving) bowl*	die Schale,
jug	der Krug
tea pot *(small)*	das Teekännchen
tea pot *(large)*	die Teekanne
coffee pot *(small)*	das Kaffeekännchen
coffee pot *(large)*	die Kaffeekanne
(cooking) pot	der Topf

OTHER THINGS	**ANDERE SACHEN**
coaster, beer coaster/mat	der Untersetzer, der Bierdeckel

napkin, serviette	die Serviette
place setting	das Gedeck
table mat	das Set
salt/pepper shaker	der Salzstreuer/
Pfefferstreuer	

Lesson 18

Eating and Drinking

This chapter introduces: *(1)* food words and vocabulary for eating, drinking and grocery shopping, *(2)* expressions related to those topics and *(3)* related German grammar.

Read and study the following dialogue.

LERNTIPP: You will comprehend and learn this dialogue better if you use this German-only version as much as possible, only turning to the dual-language version when you need to. You can easily switch between the two. Also, see the glossary at the bottom of the dialogue.

Your goal is to get to the point where you can read this German dialogue with full comprehension.

Dialogue 1: In der Küche - In the Kitchen

Katrin: Mutti, was machst du denn da? Ist das Wienerschnitzel?

Mutter: Ja, dein Lieblingsessen natürlich.

Katrin: Toll!

Mutti: Aber Katrin, ich habe gerade entdeckt, dass wir keine Kartoffeln für die Pommes frites haben. Kannst du mir schnell Kartoffeln bei EDEKA holen?

An der Kasse
bei EDEKA.

At the check-out
at EDEKA.

Katrin: Ja, das kann ich. Brauchst du sonst noch etwas?

Mutter: Wenn es ein paar schöne Gurken gibt, wäre das auch gut.

Katrin: Und Brötchen?

Mutter: Nein, das haben wir schon.

Katrin: OK, dann bin ich gleich wieder da.

Mutter: Hast du etwas Geld?

Katrin: Ja, genug, um ein paar Kartoffeln und Gurken zu kaufen.

Mutter: Natürlich bekommst du das Geld von mir zurück.

Katrin: Es geht schon, Mutti. Tschüs!

GLOSSARY: **wäre**=would be, **nein**=no, **e Gurke**=cucumber, **genug**=enough

Note : The letter 'e' denotes that the definite article for 'gurke' is die.

EDEKA is a German co-op chain of over 10,000 neighbourhoods, independently owned grocery stores that offer a wide variety of items, sometimes including a small bakery. By using a centralized distribution system from 12 regional centres in Germany, they are better able to compete with larger supermarkets.

Where else can you buy groceries? Below is a chart of

various shopping possibilities. Although supermarkets are popular, many Germans still prefer to shop for meat, bread, pastry, fruit and vegetables in specialty shops: the butcher, the baker, the green grocer and other specialised types of stores.

Wo kaufe ich das?
Useful words and expressions in English and German

Lebensmittel - Groceries

WO (where)	WAS *(what)*
der Supermarkt the supermarket im Supermarkt at the supermarket	fast alles almost everything die Lebensmittel groceries das Gemüse vegetables das Obst fruit die Milch milk der Käse cheese
der Bäcker the baker **beim Bäcker at the baker's** **die Bäckerei bakery**	das Brot bread das Brötchen roll die Semmeln rolls *(So. Germany, Austria)* die Torte cake der Kuchen cake
der Fleischer the butcher* **die Fleischerei butcher shop** **beim Fleischer at the butcher's**	der Fisch fish das Fleisch meat das Rindfleisch (beef)
der Metzger the butcher	das Geflügel poultry
die Metzgerei the butcher shop	das Kalbfleisch (veal)
beim Metzger at the butcher's	der Schinken ham das Schweinefleisch
pork sausage	die Wurst

*The German terms for 'butcher' and 'butcher shop' are regional. Metzger tends to be used more in southern

Germany, while Fleischer is more common in the north. The official term for the trade is Fleischer. Older, rarely used terms are Fleischhacker, Fleischhauer and Schlachter.

der Getränkemarkt
beverage shop
Here you buy beverages *(beer, coke, mineral water, etc.) by the case.*
Supermarkets now usually have a similar department.

Getränke
beverages
das Getränk beverage, drink
das Bier beer
der Wein wine
die Limonade lemonade
die Cola coke das Mineralwasser mineral water

der Markt the market
der Tante-Emma-Laden
corner market die Tankstelle selling
everything from groceries

alternative to regular

A growing trend in Germany is the gas station mini-mart, gas station *(market)*
to videos and CDs. It offers shoppers an
stores that by law are closed on Sundays and after 8pm, if not earlier.